MARCUS, IRVING H
LINES ABOUT WINE  S0-CBS-907
(4) 1971 WL 818
1004 03 674910 01 3 (IC=2)

B100403674910013B

SONOMA COUNTY
LIBRARY

OFFICIAL
DISCARD

Sonoma County

Wine Library

From the
San Francisco Vintners Club

LINES
about
WINES

from the typewriter of

IRVING H. MARCUS

Lines About Wines

© 1971 by Wine Publications

Berkeley, California

ACKNOWLEDGEMENTS

I would like to acknowledge my debt to the following for their part in getting this book together. There is Suzanne, an accomplished artist, who looked at my preliminary drawings and was honest enough to say of many, "Throw them out," which I did. There is Harriet, a professional editor who read much of the copy in galley form and was kind enough not to complain because I was so slow in getting back to her that she eventually had to re-read the material before discussing it with me. There are the former readers of my column in Wines & Vines who, when I first announced this book as a project some time back, sent in their checks, thus obligating me to complete my side of the bargain. And there is Betty, my wife, who managed to persuade me to keep at the job until the book was finished — and did it without nagging. To all these, my gratitude.

DEDICATION

To the many individuals
I now call friend
who might still be strangers
were it not
for our mutual interest
in wine.

PREFACE

This is a unique book.

It isn't merely that the author expresses opinions; authors must express opinions. What is unique in this particular volume is that the author's opinions, selected for presentation here from among editorials he has directed to the American wine industry over the past decade and more, have enduring value.

Rereading them now, we find some stating those self evident truths which we too frequently forget, with others expressing less obvious but equally true facts about the wine industry and wine in general. Serious subjects all, yet often leavened with a welcome touch of wit.

Here and there, the author is regretful and, occasionally, angry or indignant. Overall, he shows himself to be an idealist and an optimist about wine's future, especially that of table wine.

Not all of the author's battles ended in victory. But all have the imprint of Irving "Brick" Marcus' inquiring mind and insistent but not innocent questioning.

These writings are like a glass of good wine; they 'satisfy.

MAYNARD A. AMERINE
University of California at Davis

CONTENTS

INTRODUCTION

THIS is an opinionated book.

It has to be, not only because it deals with wine and there's almost no such thing as anyone connected with wine not having opinions, but also because its contents are editorials written by me for the wine industry publication, *Wines & Vines,* and if an editorial doesn't offer an opinion, it obviously isn't an editorial. The expressed opinions are, naturally, mine.

It is unlikely that there is anyone in the entire U. S. wine industry who has been in full agreement with all the editorials I have written in the past quarter century. It is equally unlikely that any single editorial has in its day won approval of all the vintners. But in the main, I think I am safe in saying that the views and the opinions I express in the selected editorials that compose this volume reflect, to a greater or lesser degree, the views and the opinions of the American wine industry.

The editorials offered here were selected from among several hundred for a variety of reasons.

First, because they deal either not at all or only on a limited basis with strictly intra-industry matters.

Second, because I felt that persons not directly connected with the wine industry might enjoy reading them.

Third, because I hoped that some readers would find some editorials thought-provoking on a non-world-shaking scale (the world is shaky enough without my contributing my bit).

Fourth, because non industry readers might learn something

from them and so get a better understanding of what winemaking is all about.

Fifth, because there is the possibility that their publication might bring in an honest dollar or two.

And finally, because their initial appearance in a monthly magazine meant that each had a life span of only thirty days or so, and I thought that binding them together might give me a sense of their having value extending beyond the comparative moment of their original reading.

I think this latter is an excusable egocentricity, since if I didn't believe the editorials had something to say, I wouldn't have written them.

So much for this being an opinionated book. It is also a biased book.

Aside from the fact that each of us is biased according to his background and upbringing, I have a particular bias in favor of the wine industry of this country and this, I am certain, shows through in the following pages.

I am not, however, blindly biased. I do not think that all our vintners are paragons of virtue, or pure artists, or even the best winemakers in the world. I do not believe that, *per se,* a high priced American wine is automatically the equal of, or better than, its European counterpart, just as I don't believe that a wine carrying a foreign label is, for that reason alone, automatically one of the best wines in the world.

I simply contend that there are fine wines made in France, in Germany, in Italy, in practically every wine producing nation in the world, *including* the United States.

This last point is, I've found, lost sight of by some of the people some of the time, and I feel it my duty to remind them of it occasionally.

If this isn't bias, let the psychiatrists make the most of it.

Now, as to the title of this book. "Lines About Wines" was a phrase used by a San Francisco radio station a couple of years or so back to introduce its occasional sentence or two on wine or wine imbibing. I liked it because it had a swing. So I purloined it.

I liked it, too, because it fitted the pattern in which my editorials are presented in *Wines & Vines,* with each editorial consisting of a specific and non-varying number of lines, and with the lines being unequal in length.

The reason for this odd manner of presenting editorials is that, some years ago, I had a very imaginative layout man redesign the format of the magazine, and his specifications were exact.

His idea (I believe he had just celebrated his 41st birthday) was that the editorial should have 41 uneven lines, with no line having more than 66 characters. (Sixty-six characters in search of an author?)

Oh, I argued with him. It's hard enough, I told him, to get a worthwhile editorial idea. It is harder still to put the idea into an unlimited number of lines in order to get the reader reaction sought after. Why make a tough job even tougher by limiting the editorial to a specific number of lines, and uneven lines at that?

It looks good on the page, was the answer.

I appreciate the value of visual impression, so I agreed.

While this editorial form, I told myself, is certainly an artificial one, is it, for example, more artificial than the sonnet form? Obviously not, and if Shakespeare and Shelley and Keats (all non-wine-industry writers) could get imaginative ideas over in the artificial measures of a sonnet, then I should be able to get over in this less stringent form whatever lesser ideas I might have.

So that's the way it began.

With minor changes, none of which alter the sense of the editorials, the pieces proffered here are exactly as published during the indicated month. Many of them, in fact, are simply photographed reproductions from the magazine. There is, however, one change made repeatedly in the texts of the earlier editorials about which I'd like to comment because it involved a change of writing style which may seem minor to you but not to me.

Like most editorial writers of the old school, I was long in the habit of using the editorial "we." But some half dozen years ago, I decided to modernize myself and changed to the first person singular, the "perpendicular pronoun," as someone aptly called it. Therefore editorials from before January 1964 have had the editorial plural of their original presentation singularized.

In the presented editorials, you will note time gaps—a month, three months, even at the beginning a year or so—between suc-

17

cessive items. This does not mean there were no editorials during those missing periods. It's simply that the editorials presented in those months dealt with matters so intra-industry that a reader not acquainted with what was going on among the vintners at that time would simply wonder what all the fuss was about.

Since the editorials necessarily refer to situations current a varying number of months or years back, I was pleased on re-reading them before sending them on to the printer to find I can still live with most of the conclusions I reached. Even in those cases where I may today come up with a different answer on a particular subject, the individual editorial published here is valid because it reflects my reaction to the *then* situation.

This *then*, you will note, encompasses mainly the decade of the 1960s, now a matter of history but still not ancient history. I found it interesting that, in no single year of that busy decade, could I with logic select all twelve monthly editorials for presentation here. There are, however, a substantial number of years in which eleven of the editorials seemed to me to warrant publication.

One other matter and I'll cut this off.

When I first thought of doing this book, I placed a number of editorials in the hands of an artist, asking her to illustrate them. After some weeks, she returned them—without even a rough pencil sketch to show.

"The ideas are there," she said, "but they don't lend themselves to illustration."

This was a shocker. I stewed about it for a while, then one weekend I took out some of the editorials, picked up a soft pencil and a piece of drawing paper, and tried to rough out some illustrations. When I had done a half dozen or so, I concluded that they showed graphically the essence of what the editorial said in words, and if they didn't show it in a professional manner, that was just too bad, because that's how they were going to appear. You may scorn them as art, but frankly I'm as proud of them as Matisse must have been of his own first efforts—assuming these took place when he was three.

Now I'm finally through with this preamble. I only wish I could have fitted it into 41 lines.

VIN ORDINAIRE

The man who says, "There's no accounting for tastes,"
is likely a snob who believes he belongs to that elite few
whose tastes—of course!—are superior to those of the many.

He may be right, he may be wrong; no sense arguing about taste.
A number of firms don't argue. They deliberately cater to the
presumably sophisticated taste (and substantial purse) of the few.
But for those seeking business on a larger scale, such an approach
is wrong; they must satisfy the taste and purse of the many.

In wine, the taste of the non-connoisseur majority usually differs from that of the connoisseur. (Mind you, I'm making no judgement as to which is "right"; I'm only saying that the two differ.) In the face of such an obvious truth, it is hardly conceivable that, up to a few years ago, it was the connoisseur who was asked to decide what would be a good wine for the U.S. mass market.

U. S. volume winemakers used to produce mainly what you could call traditional type wines, then had them rated by connoisseur–judges according to how "true to type" they were—the type in each case being the particular wine's European forebear. Completely lost or overlooked was the fact that most U. S. residents, while also possessing European forebears, were themselves not "true to type."

What may have opened many vintners' eyes were the dramatic gains made by the Concord wines in the late 1940s—wines which the European-faceted connoisseur scorned but which thousands liked. Facing the facts, a number of volume producers then began developing new wines aimed at pleasing the taste of the majority. If the nation's connoisseurs were also pleased, so much the better, but the main target among these producers was to make wines that would appeal to the greatest possible number of Americans.

Out of this effort came the popular priced rosés, the growth of the mellow reds, the softening of American table wines generally. Out of this came the production of wines to "go with everything." And perhaps most importantly, out of this came the determination to end the aura of mystery surrounding wine and wine service.

While the industry has not yet reached that laudable last goal, it is surely moving in that direction. For this, you and I should pay homage to those aggressive vintners who, years back, took as their credo: "Find out what the average man likes and make it."

I know. There's no such thing as an average man. Yet it is this same non-average "average" man who so often calls the turn on how a product, a firm, an industry (even a nation!) is to go.

Which is why I applaud *vin ordinaire* for man *ordinaire*.

JUNE, 1956

TOUCHDOWN

When I was considerably younger, I played some football
under a coach whose code was, "The best defense is an offense."
California vintners now seem to have accepted the soundness
of this theme. Certainly, within the past year or so,
they've changed from disorganized defense to sound offense.

Before making this move, the premium producers of California
used to spend considerable time crying, "Foul!" when publicized
comments of foreign producers, importers or their representatives
left the impression on the public that "Yes, in California
there are some nice little wines, but as for the real thing . . ."

Now, these same California vintners are saying in essence,
"Yes, there are a number of fine foreign wines — too."
And now it is the importers who are crying, "Foul!"

Why? Because the California vintners asked groups of people to evaluate some California and foreign wines without revealing beforehand which was which, and then let it be known — as was actually the case — that the California wines outscored the foreign wines as often as not.

"It's not fair," the importers complained in substance — and complained not only to each other but to Washington as well. "It's not fair to let the California vintners tell the people that their wines scored as well as ours!"

Why not? It happened. Moreover it happened with a variety of groups in a variety of U.S. cities. It happened with a panel of known connoisseurs, with another panel of wine wholesalers, and with still a third panel of retailers. It happened with separate panels of newspapermen and magazine editors — it even happened with a panel of importers!

The tastings were not "stacked." They included — in set turn, mind you — the labels of various California premium wines, matched against some of the accepted "best" of foreign brands.

Moreover, most of the participants — and this is a reflection of the public attitude the Californians are fighting — began the tastings with a strong bias in favor of the foreign product.

Why, then, isn't it fair to let the public in on the facts? California vintners had always said they had some fine wines. Now they are simply saying it more frequently, more aggressively and more believably. Now they are getting others — including former doubting Thomases — to support them in their contention that, yes, their fine wines can match Europe's fine wines.

Now they are carrying the ball.

AUGUST, 1956

NO BED OF ROSES

WITH your permission, I'd like to take back some of the things
I've written in this column during the past several years.
Like many others, I've complained a lot about the handicaps
which hem in vintners' selling efforts. What I griped about
particularly was the fact that many of the merchandising
practices accepted as normal in other fields are denied
the wine industry. While I haven't changed my mind completely
on this subject, I'm not nearly as sure as I used to be
that every selling limitation is necessarily a handicap.

What helped bring about this change of attitude was a recent radio plug for a new detergent: "The manufacturer of this detergent," said the radio announcement, "*will pay you 25 cents* just for trying it."

All the buyer had to do was to mail a coupon from the package to the detergent manufacturer and, like manna from heaven, back would come a shiny 25 cent piece.

With all the miserable limitations currently holding back the merchandising of wine, the vintners should at least be happy that they aren't faced with the possibility (and don't think somebody wouldn't do it!) that one or more of their numbers would offer to return a dime or a quarter or a half dollar of the purchase price to anybody willing to try a particular brand or type of wine.

Consider, too, that with the right to merchandise wine as other items are merchandised, there would be no limit to "things of value" that could be offered retailers, or even consumers.

How about a deal in which two bottles of wine would sell for the price of one, plus one cent? How about coupons which could be redeemed for ten cents on the next purchase of a wine? How about a selling gimmick in which a bottle of Dry Vermouth is given away free with every two bottles of gin purchased?

Obviously, there are headaches in merchandising regardless of whether selling procedures are restricted or not.

I still think the wine industry is being unfairly dealt with in many directions. I continue to believe that the producers, the trade and the public would be better off if some of the unwarranted limitations on wine merchandising were removed. But I am far from sure that the right to merchandise wine as if it were coffee or soap or napkins would automatically guarantee that every sale would be made at a profit.

Maybe I've learned something.

FEBRUARY, 1957

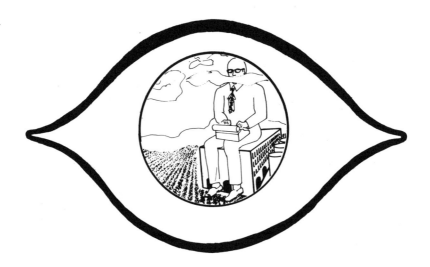

BELIEVING IS SEEING

EVERY industry needs a vocal idealist, and it seems in the nature
of things that the editor of an industry publication
should take that role.

Actually, I've played the part of wine industry idealist for
many years. But in pursuit of my job as I see it, I think
I've managed to mix in a little practicality with my ideals.

Doing this is something like trying to keep your head
in the clouds and your feet on the ground at the same time.
It's a neat trick if you can do it without getting either stars
in your eyes or cold feet, and maybe I haven't managed it
every time.

One thing is certain: this approach gives one a sort of double vision. You see the accomplished good, but you always see it shadowed by the less-than-good.

Here, as examples, are some of the things I see when I look at the wine industry today:

* An industry which has grown substantially in the past twenty years (but which is not as big as it should be).

* A real gain in merchandising concepts compared to the casual approach of the 1930's (but still far behind the accepted standards in many industries).

* A strong interest on the part of the vintners in bettering the quality of grapes crushed (but with some independent growers resenting the downgrading of the loads they send the vintners).

* A growing willingness on the part of the public to accept the idea that U. S. vintners can produce top quality wines (but with plenty of doubting voices still raised in public).

* A better understanding of the type of wine the average U. S. resident is likely to favor (but with no real follow through to establish these likes with reasonable certainty).

* A recognition that the public has to be "educated" to wine use (but a reluctance to put up the funds to get this job done).

The above gives you an idea of how schizophrenic a practical idealist can be. He gets the good and the bad all mixed together, and in the end he doesn't know whether to applaud the industry for what it has accomplished, or to criticize it for what it has failed to do.

Usually, he decides that he has underestimated the good and overemphasized the bad, and comes to the conclusion that it's a wonderful industry, after all.

This is the sure sign of the idealist.

AUGUST, 1957

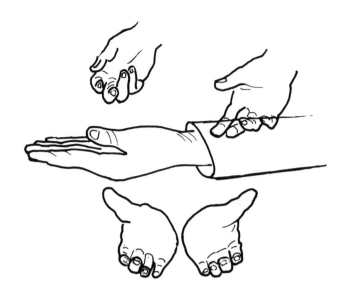

. . . AND CHARITY

I've never met one personally, but there may well be a vintner
who's never been asked to donate a number of bottles or cases
to a worthy cause. If you are one such, you can skip this.
You're free of what seems to me to be a real problem.

I have no quarrel with worthy causes and I greatly admire
those who spend their time doing good. But from the evidence,
I can only conclude that American vintners are on the sucker list
of a substantial number of organizations seeking a gimmick
to attract greater numbers to one of their gatherings.

I recognize there are times when it is to the advantage
of a winery to have its products served at some social function.
It's one of the better ways to get a brand more widely known
and it helps win appreciation for the quality of a firm's wines.
So, generally, the vintners don't mind a reasonable number
of requests for a reasonable number of cases.

Obviously, though, a businessman must set limits on free goods, regardless of the worthiness of the cause or of the people asking for wine. (It is unfortunate but true that requests for free wine often come from some whose only connection with charity appears to be that which they ask of the vintners themselves.) Yet when a vintner, having done more than his share of giving, tells a group, "Sorry," he is open to becoming *persona non grata* and his wine *vino non grata* with that organization's members.

On occasion, when I have become aware of some group or other proposing to put on, say, a banquet or dinner to raise funds for a particular reason, I've tried to check out just what is being donated to the affair. My snooping usually shows that the sponsoring group pays full price for the banquet hall, full price for the meal and full price for the music, if any. The only thing the group seems to expect to get free is the wine. I suppose that if, over a period of time, people stopped asking a vintner to donate his products, he would start worrying. Is he on the black list? Have his wines lost their social appeal? I can see where he would be faced with a real or fancied problem.

It is quite possible that requests for donations of wine are not the bugaboo I consider them, and indeed there may be vintners who gladly embrace any and all occasions to give away that which they're in business to sell. Such vintners, I'm sure will have no trouble finding a ready market for their free goods. If this satisfies them, all I can do is to applaud them for charity above and beyond the call of duty.

DECEMBER, 1958

29

A WORK OF ART

CRASS commercialism enters into practically everyone's life, even into the lives of those individualists who exist in the sometime ivory tower-ish world of art.

True, when an artist puts paint to canvas, or a sculptor shapes a statue or a composer writes his imaginative musical notations or a dancer develops the fluid movements of her profession, artistic ideals are primarily in mind.

But idealistic as the artist may be, a certain amount of practicality enters into his measure of his work. This is particularly true when he wins an award or comes in first in a competition. He is proud of the medal or the honor—but he is also well aware that public knowledge of that award can increase his prestige, leading to greater acceptance of, and a higher price for, his artistic efforts.

So it is with the art of producing wine.

Honors, in terms of awards won at competitions, are fine. They make the producer feel that people of discernment are appreciative of his efforts. But, in the opinion of some vintners, if the honors cannot lead to wider acceptance of the art product, they are empty honors.

In other words, why enter the competitions and win medals if you can't put those medals to work building sales?

This is a touchy subject in the industry. Yet, with the 1959 awards published and with a number of wineries plugging their successes in ads and releases, comment is timely.

Maybe the best way to start is to note that, as far as my observations go, every winner at past competitions (and this includes those not now participating) has in some fashion or other taken commercial advantage of the medals won by his wines.

Even the hanging of a medal in a winery showcase where
visitors can see it, is in essence a merchandising effort,
though a muted one.

So it is not completely a problem of *not* using the awards
to the winery's advantage, but HOW the awards are used.

I believe a prize winner has the right to use whatever means
he feels are needed to let the trade and the public know
that competent judges have admired the artistry of his work.
If this can be labeled as commercialism, what of it?
Granting that the production of fine wine is an art,
isn't it equally—and primarily—a business venture?

SEPTEMBER, 1959

PARTNERS

THERE are some things, like playing a game of tennis or becoming a parent, you simply can't do all by yourself. The California wine industry, in its efforts to better the already high quality of grapes that go into its crushers, is likely to find this out during the coming vintage.

It's history how the vintners—with, shall we say, the encouragement of Food & Drug—underwrote a project some three years ago to obtain data on defects in grapes delivered the wineries, and to devise ways to measure such defects.

This program has moved ahead very well indeed—to a point. The vintners have obtained the data they sought, they have developed a practical mechanical sampler for bulk loads, and last year they instituted a voluntary third-person inspection system for grapes delivered to the crushers. These are all impressive forward steps.

The ideal towards which the industry is marching is the achievement of "perfect" fruit for making into wine. Nature being what it is, there are both vintners and growers who will wager any sum that no such thing is possible for an entire crop or even for a substantial portion.

Granting the fact that perfection can't be achieved, the question arises as to whether the vintners can, by their lone efforts, reach the practical equivalent. The answer seems to be no.

Obviously, the basic job has to be done in the vineyards, not at the inspection stations near the crushers. While the 100,000 acres or so of vineyards operated by the vintners are likely to receive particular attention in meeting the stricter winery standards, there is not at all the same assurance about the vineyards run by independent growers from whom the vintners will buy.

This is where the vintner finds he must have an ally. This is where he realizes he can't go it alone.

The grape growers must be made sharply aware of the needs of the vintner, and must be persuaded to meet those needs. Certainly, the vintner has a mighty forceful persuader in his right to turn down loads not found up to standard. But a better way is to work *with* the grower, to limit as far as possible the need for turning down loads, and to make the man in the vineyard a willing partner rather than a reluctant and antagonistic participant.

FEBRUARY, 1960

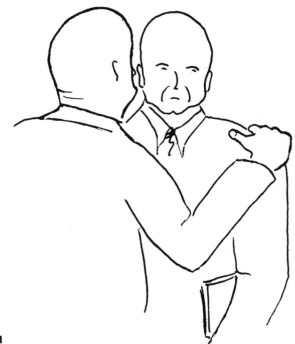

SH-H!

SH-H. Come over here a minute. I'm going to let you in
on a little secret. I've just been checking the facts
on the dessert wine situation. They all point to one thing:
Dessert wines are going no place fast, and . . .
Oh. You knew about it already.
And you think it's poor advertising that's to blame?
Well, I don't know about that. My theory is . . .
You have to go? Well, maybe we can get together later.

Sh-h. Let's get over in this corner. This is hot.
I've been checking dessert wine sales and, believe me,
the evidence is that they're going nowhere at all . . .
Oh. So you knew it, too.
You say it's the economic situation that's at fault?
Things are just too good for the average man to think about
dessert wine when he buys an alcoholic beverage?
Could be. But my theory is . . .
You're late for an appointment? Sure, go right ahead.

Sh-h. Hold it a minute. Look at these dessert wine figures.
Do you realize what they mean? I tell you I studied them
for a full day and I came to the conclusion that . . .
Oh. You've already checked the figures.
You think it's the Flavored Wines that caused the drop?
They're simply causing the dessert wine drinker to switch?
I'm not saying you're not right, but my theory is . . .
You're busy now? Well, I'll drop in at your office tomorrow.

Wonder why it's so tough to get my theory on this across?
Seems to me that the main point is simple enough:
If dessert wines were as appealing to the public as some
suppose them to be, then advertising would be much more
effective, good times wouldn't bring the volume down,
and there wouldn't BE any switching to the Flavored Wines
or to any other alcoholic beverage. The way I look at it,
when a consumer's satisfied with the beverage he drinks,
you just can't get him to switch. Try to get a Bourbon man
to switch to Scotch. See what I mean?

So my theory is that maybe the traditional dessert wines
don't offer what the current market wants. If this is right,
then maybe it's a good thing we've got the Flavored Wines.
At least we're keeping the consumer as a *wine* drinker
instead of letting him switch to some non-vinous product, and . . .
What did you say? I see. Well, what's YOUR theory?

MAY, 1960

A MESSAGE TO OMAR

YOU remember Omar Khayyam
You know: "A loaf of bread, a jug of wine and thou . . ."
Well, in that same poem, which so aptly sings the praises of wine,
Omar goes on to say: "I wonder often what the vintners buy,
One half so precious as the stuff they sell."
A wonderfully poetic thought.

I have been pondering these oft-quoted lines,
and while I don't know what the vintner bought in Omar's day,
I have come up with a fact or two on what the modern vintner buys
that may be an unpoetic surprise to present day Omars.

36

For one rather obvious thing, the vintner buys grapes.
Or if he is one who grows his own grapes, then he buys fertilizers
and weed killers and irrigation equipment and sprayers
and all those dozens of material and unromantic things he needs
to see that the grapes grow up to become wine.

For another, grape grower or not, the vintner as a winemaker
buys presses and crushers to squeeze the juice from the grapes,
casks and tanks to age the wine, laboratory equipment to test
the wine, unscramblers and fillers and cappers and labelers
to package the wine, bottles and labels and corks and foils
to dress up the package—and advertising space to advise
people that the wine is good enough to write a poem about.

Then, too, the vintner buys knowledge; the experience of men.
Men to work the vineyards, fight the bugs, assess the grapes;
men to decide what grapes should be used for what wines;
men to judge the wines as they mature, to evaluate them,
to decide when they should be packaged, when shipped;
men to do the unromantic but necessary jobs of running the
office and the shipping room and the trucking department;
men to persuade other men to place the wine on their shelves
so as to make them available to the poets and other customers.

Moreover, the vintner has to buy the right to do business.
He buys licenses and permits, pays fees and assessments.
And as for taxes, he's faced with county, state and Federal;
real property, personal property, social security, sales;
even, if he's lucky, income taxes.

As you see, Omar, the vintner has plenty to buy with his money.
If some of these things appear crass to you, I'm sorry.
Without wanting to be cruelly critical, it appears from your poem
that you're likely living somewhere out of this world.
It was nevertheless a very nice thought you had. Thank you.

JUNE, 1960

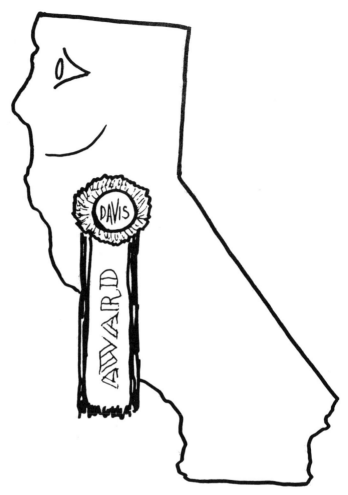

AWARD WINNER

CONSIDER the case of the award-winning Australian enologist
who recently decided to spend his awarded year of grace
on the campus of the University of California at Davis.
As news in a U. S. wine industry publication, this is worth
perhaps two or three paragraphs at the most.
On this page, the story is not news; it's a symbol.

Think a moment. Here was a highly respected enologist, the manager of the Viticultural Research Station of the South Australian government, who suddenly found himself with a prize of £1500 to be used as he desired for a year of study in his field anywhere in the world. Open to him were the research stations of France, Germany, Italy, Spain and other grape and wine producing nations (and in all these countries the award money would go further than in the U. S.). Yet, with the world to choose from, he selected California!

That he did so is not as surprising as the above exclamation point implies. Over the years, other Australians—and French and Germans and Swiss and what-have-you, have done the same.

The reason is simple: The research work being done on the Davis campus of the University in viticulture and enology is of world stature; in both fields, the University's faculty is recognized as among the best. Their published research efforts are studied and used to advantage in many of the older winemaking countries. From time to time, some of them are called to Europe for consultation on vintner problems. What better mark of stature?

I'm revealing no secret in saying that the University's enological and viticultural researchers, who have rarely failed to find a solution to the varied problems dropped in their laps, are pretty much taken for granted in this country, where we have the tendency to ask the impossible of our research men and then wait impatiently for them to get the job done.

It is good, therefore, that from time to time some external evaluation of their work is brought to our attention. No greater measure of the standing of the University people can be found than that one of their kind from another nation should select them as the preferred men from whom to learn.

It is true that the Rudi Buring Award was deservedly won by Australia's Harold William Tulloch, R.D.A., R.D. Oen. Yet, in the final analysis, the real award fell to the University of California.

JULY, 1960

FIGHT!

NOBODY in his right mind goes around looking for a fight.
But if you're in the wine business (or any other business,
for that matter) you're in a fight *automatically*.
The question being investigated here is whether or not
you're prepared to put up a good fight.

Consider: You're at the beginning of a New Year—or in
view of the subject matter here, maybe we should call it a
New Round. When that round ends, some 365 days later,
some of you will have won it. *Some* of you.

To get your hand raised as a winner depends mostly on you.
That your opponents will be tough, you can be sure.
But whether your opposition takes the form of bigger ad budgets
than yours, or bulk prices below the level of reason,
or unending floods of foreign wines, or salesmen from competing
firms who seem to work 28-hour days, or any of a dozen other
unrelenting, pressing shapes—well, that's what you're up against,
and that's what you've got to beat in order to win, period.

Am I suggesting the impossible?

Am I asking that you be a David versus a Goliath,
a financial genius, a merchandising magician, a super-salesman
more super than any the wine industry has yet seen?

Maybe I am.

But if I am, it's because I feel this is the only way
you or anyone can make the grade. If you mean to see 1961
and the other fast-crowding years through as a business man
or business firm, this is most assuredly no time for hesitating,
no time for withdrawing, no time for showing what amounts
to commercial cowardice.

In the commercial world, security for job or business
is bought only at the price of constant aggressiveness.
And for those who look beyond security to advancement,
the price is twice as high.

This is hardly a new thought. But its application
to the wine industry of today can't be seriously challenged.

Such being the case, it doesn't take a medium
to envision the fast approaching year
as one which will call for you to clench your fists
and start punching. Hard.
For, whether you're looking for it or not,
1961 is likely to bring you the fight of your life.

Maybe even the fight FOR your life.

DECEMBER, 1960

41

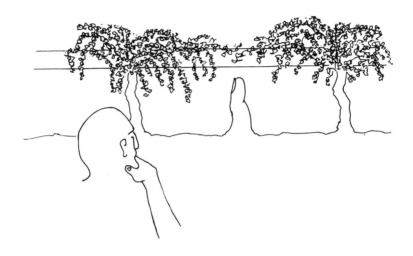

GREEN THUMB

WHEN it comes to growing grapes commercially,
the "green thumb" of which so many home gardeners
speak so highly is not much more than an empty phrase.
Assuming Nature provides the proper weather conditions
(quite an assumption in some parts of the world
and in some years), the successful growing of grapes
for market is today a matter of applied science,
not of "intuitive" care of grape vines.

The growers, with the aid of the viticulturists
(and of the entomologists and the pestologists and the
nematologists, etc., etc.), can now make more and better grapes
grow on an acre of land than ever before.

This is generally looked upon as a good thing.
But there have been occasions in the past
(and there are likely to be occasions in the future)
when the growers, the vintners, the fresh grape shippers
and the raisin packers have all been acutely embarrassed
by the generosity of the vines.

This generosity doesn't necessarily extend to money.
When the vines are prodigal, it is in terms of tonnage,
while what the grower really intended to plant was income.
Big tonnage is only too often offset by low per-ton returns;
and it doesn't require a mathematical genius to figure out
that ten tons of grapes to the acre at $31.50 per ton
is no more money in the pocket than seven tons at $45.

That ten tons of grapes can now be made to grow where
only seven grew before (and three tons where a mere 1½ tons
grew before) is obviously not the ultimate answer.

That answer lies in creating an expanding market for grapes
and for the various grape products. In this direction,
the wine industry, while it has by no means achieved anything
like the goal it set for itself a couple of decades back,
is still the *only* grape market that has expanded at all.
Willy-nilly, then, the grower's fate is bound to that of the vintner.

Scientific pruning, fertilizing, irrigating and harvesting
may give the grower all the earmarks of a man with a green thumb,
but until the wine market moves ahead substantially
(and this is perhaps something not every grower understands),
no agricultural scientist can show the vineyardist how to produce
that one crop he universally hopes to harvest year after year
—big money.

FEBRUARY, 1961

RICHER, POORER

ONLY a few people can afford to be rich.
I don't mean rich in ideas, in talent, in friends, in memories
—all of which are quite properly highly regarded.
I mean RICH, like in money.

In California, one of the best ways to be rich is to own land,
and this very month I have concrete evidence that,
if you own the right amount of land in the right place,
you're really so rich that you can't afford to stay in business.

This, basically, is what is happening to Garrett & Company,
vineyardists and vintners of Southern California.

For the past several months, a highly recognized firm of
financial counselors has been studying the Garrett operation,
and early this month came the announcement
that, with all the very valuable land the firm owns,
it's economically silly for this substantial company
to continue to grow grapes and make wine for a living.

It wasn't put in quite those words, naturally,
but it couldn't have been spelled out more clearly.

To be rather blunt about it, the matter of land values
is only a part of the Garrett story, though an important part.
For the rest, it must be considered that Garrett has for some
time been losing its marketing position, that the firm
hasn't shown the necessary merchandising agressiveness—
and that the expenditure of time, money, and effort involved
in trying to get Garrett back into the competitive stream
was likely too much for the firm's officials to contemplate.

Given different circumstances, in which there weren't
some few millions just waiting to be gathered fondly in,
it's conceivable that the Garrett officers would have taken
the necessary steps, would have once again become
real merchandisers, would have tried to fight back to a
position in which reasonable profits were possible.
But with all that land worth all that money . . . ?

My real concern is not so much that Garrett is closing
its doors, though it's sad to lose a venerable industry member.
What has me worried more is the number of other wineries
—in Cucamonga, Santa Clara, Napa, etc.—which may,
in this decade, literally be forced to shut up shop
for the same reason. If this happens, California will soon
have the richest bunch of ex-vintners in the world
—and the wine industry will be the poorer for it.

APRIL, 1961

WCTU

EVER been a minority of one?
I had this experience early this month, as I wandered among
members of the Women's Christian Temperance Union
who were convening a mere 100 yard dash from this office.
I haven't quite recovered.

Walking through the convention hotel corridors as the
motherly looking delegates gathered, checking the exhibit hall
and reading the literature, sitting in at some meetings and
sensing the sincerity with which the Madam Chairwoman and others
denounced Demon Rum, disturbed me—but not quite in the
way the delegates would want me to be disturbed.

The emotion I felt, in all honesty, was pity.
For here was a group of apparently intelligent women,
mostly of gray-hair or white-hair maturity,
who were embarked with full sincerity on a program based
on a false premise: that to make alcoholic beverages illegal,
was to do away with alcoholic beverages.

This is of course utter nonsense, as Prohibition proved;
and actually, it seems that the WCTU recognizes
there's small chance of achieving national Prohibition again.

It has therefore turned to lesser but more immediate goals,
including that of advocating individual prohibition; a sort of
person-to-person persuasive effort to promote total abstinence.
And here, I think, the ladies make their big mistake.

The chance of persuading any considerable number of citizens
to *abstain* from using a product that the general public
accepts as normal and seems to enjoy using, is pretty slim.
So I've come up with an idea that may be the saving of this
venerable organization, of which I, wrong sex and all,
now consider myself a sort of ex-officio member.

The idea is simplicity itself. Let the members face up
to reality; let them forget about Prohibition, a lost cause;
let them give up their attempts to persuade adults to live
without alcohol; let them be more practical and do a
considerably bigger job—teach people to live *with* alcohol.

Doing this, the WCTU may find itself actually accomplishing
something worthwhile. It may also find that its arch enemies,
the alcoholic beverage industries, have become its friends.
For the people of these industries—and most certainly,
those in the wine industry—truly want and seek *Temperance*.

It's most unfortunate that the WCTU apparently does not.

AUGUST, 1961

47

TO SEE OURSELVES

IN spite of Robert Burns' poetic and oft-quoted lines
on how wonderful it would be to see ourselves as others see us,
it's doubtful that many of us would dare take a look.
But, on the basis that a man is what he does,
a number of industry job holders in California's coastal
counties vineyards and wineries recently got the chance
to see themselves through others' eyes.

The eyes belonged to the California Department of Employment,
which set out a year ago to apply a realistic yardstick
to four industry jobs, for the purpose of publishing
a "Guide" for each job that would be just that
to persons looking toward such posts for their lifetime work.

When these Guides, which deal with the viticulturist, enologist,
vineyard manager, and cellar foreman, came across my desk,
I felt it my reportorial duty to summarize their findings.
But the Guides also aroused my curiosity as an editor—mainly
because the recent American Society of Enologists convention
featured a symposium in which some enologists, viticulturists,
and employers took the rostrum in turn, in an attempt to do
more or less the same evaluative job, only from the inside.

Those who attended the ASE symposium on this subject,
or who read my summarization in *Wines & Vines,* may recall
that most of the conclusions reached by the speakers
were quite optimistic, as likely they should have been.

However, in taking notes and in writing the copy later,
I must admit that I had an uneasy feeling
that getting an enologist or the employer of an enologist
to evaluate the job in public, was perhaps not the best way
to arrive at an unbiased summation.

So, with due respect to the sincerity of those who took
part in the American Society of Enologists' symposium,
I believe that the Department of Employment Guides—
in spite of being geographically limited to certain counties—
stand as the only unbiased evaluations the industry has
of four extremely important production posts.

But before you consider how lucky the persons in these jobs
are to have an outsider's view of their work,
perhaps you should be reminded of the fact that most of us,
rather than really wanting to see ourselves as others see us,
would much prefer to arrange it that the others
should see us as we see ourselves.

MESSAGE FOR WCTU

Ladies, I have good news for you:
the people of the United States are becoming more temperate.
While there may be a slightly greater amount of alcohol
consumed than there was, say, a dozen years ago,
there is a very definite trend to the consumption
of the more temperate—the less alcoholic—beverages.

I'm sorry I can't give you credit for this change,
but the fact of the matter is that I don't believe
your efforts in behalf of temperance are very effective
—quite likely because you're not really so much for
temperance as you are for abstinence.

Three things have happened to bring about the swing to temperance. First, though more people admittedly are drinking, each average drinker is drinking less—a step in the right direction, no?

Secondly, the alcoholic content in the spirituous beverages has been reduced. Where, a dozen years ago, it likely averaged around 90 proof (45% alcohol), it is now believed to average around 85 proof, with more and more being marketed at 80 proof. So each fifth bought averages less alcohol than it did previously.

Thirdly, and most importantly from my point of view, of all the alcoholic beverages available to the U.S. adult today, the one which is making the most impressive advance is that which, next to beer, has the *least* alcoholic content.

That's table wine, of course, which in this country can't contain more than 14% alcohol (the rest is mainly water, and surely you don't object to *that*).

Presumably, you don't even object to carbon dioxide, but just in case you do, I have deliberately excluded from my table wine total the very dramatic advances made by Champagne, which is really a table wine with natural effervescence.

In spite of this super-carefulness on my part (unusual for one trying to make a statistical point), the story of the advance of temperance in the United States should be pretty pleasant reading for you. Here are the facts.

Between 1950 and last year, the average United States adult (who of course doesn't exist but is statistically indispensible) upped his spirits drinking by a non-exciting 13% while boosting his consumption of the low-alcohol table wines by a big 43%.

Since table wine is purchased and used mainly as an acompaniment to food rather than for its alcoholic content (you can't say the same of spirits), I rate this as pretty good evidence that the people of the U. S. are moving towards real temperance.

Why not join them?

JULY, 1962

WORDS ON WINE

No. 1 theme among book authors in the United States
is unquestionably that of Boy meets Girl, a love story.
What the second, third and fourth most popular themes are,
I can't even guess. But somewhere down the line,
and not too far down at that, stands the theme of
Man meets Wine, also a love story.

Today, for example, I personally know of four writers
who are in various stages of putting together books on wine.
Inasmuch as this year has already seen the publication
of a number of volumes on this subject, why do authors
continue to write, and people continue to buy, books on wine?

Some say it's the complexity of the subject.
Only this month, Robert Alden, writing in the N. Y. Times,
noted that there are at least 1000 different vineyard names
in the Bordeaux region alone. Multiply the Bordeaux region
by the number of other wine producing areas in the world,
and you come up with a figure that only one of those
electronic monsters now replacing bookkeepers can digest.

Others say it's the romance associated with wine.
The Bible talks well of it, poets constantly glow over it,
songwriters periodically put its glories to music,
and births, weddings and anniversaries the world over
are celebrated with it. Wine is surely steeped in romance.

Still others say it's simply curiosity about wine.
The average U. S. resident, not knowing much about wine,
sees people enjoying it on the movie screen, reads about
Champagne receptions in the society columns and is exposed
to sales messages about wine wherever he turns.
If he becomes curious, he can't be blamed.

So, whether the goal be to satisfy curiosity about wine,
to glorify its romance, to clear up its complexities
or just to make money, writers always seem to be at work
putting together books about wine—or if not books,
magazine articles on the very same subject.

Is all this writing necessary? Or important?
I say yes; yes in spite of Lawton Mackall, whom you may recall
as a writer on "Potables" some years back. Mackall insisted
you could give the public all the advice it needs about wine
in three words—"You drink it." But even Mackall found
it took thousands of words to get this simple message across.

I guess that this is the real "why" of wine books.

OCTOBER, 1962

WINE LIST
RED WINES

	BOTTLE
CABERNET SAUVIGNON	$7.50
GAMAY BEAUJOLAIS	6.75
PINOT NOIR (V)	9.00
BARBERA	6.75

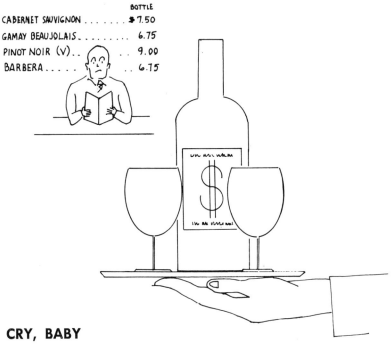

CRY, BABY

Restaurant pricing of wine is not a new subject to weep over.
Leon Adams called it "the great restaurant swindle" in his book
on wine, and more recently Richard Calvert called it even worse
in his column in *The Beverage Retailer Weekly*.

I agree with both writers. Their arguments are reasonable,
soundly based and convincing—convincing to me, that is.
Whether they would convince even one restaurateur to lower
one unreasonable wine price is something else again.

I've talked with salesmen who've tried to persuade
restaurateurs to drop excessive prices charged for their wines.
The usual reply they got was, "If you don't like my pricing,
don't sell me your wine." What salesman can fight that?

Recently, a California premium wine producer shocked members
of the Academy of Master Wine Growers (all of whom sell
restaurants and should be shock-proof on the pricing problem)
by showing them a wine list of a California restaurant
in which a particular brand, costing the restaurant
$7.70 per case, was priced at $5.50 per *bottle*.

What hurts about things of this sort is that,
when a restaurateur is trying to make a killing of this kind,
what he's really killing is the future of wine.

There are those who believe, and you can count me among them,
that the future of the wine industry in the United States
depends on how table wine (or dinner wine, if you prefer)
is accepted by the average man. It's tough to get the idea
of wine-with-food into such a man's head, and it hurts
when this idea is chased out aborning by high wine pricing,
losing a sale for both the restaurant and the industry.

As a patron, I have on occasion complained
to a restaurant manager about the pricing of his wines,
but as far as I could discover, it was just wasted breath.

I suspect the restaurateur's reaction to my complaint
would have been quite different if it had been preceded
by like grievances expressed by other dining patrons.
But with human beings being only human
(Wife to husband: "Don't you *dare* make a fuss!"),
practically nobody ever opens his mouth to complain.

Since this is so, and since it seems that industry efforts
to eliminate excessive wine pricing are getting nowhere,
the eating-out public has only itself to blame
for letting the restaurateurs get away with such pricing.

JANUARY, 1963

MONEY

They say making too much money tends to destroy moral fiber,
but this is a chance most of us would be willing to take.
Talking about making money shouldn't be too dangerous, though,
and this columnist is likely undergoing no moral risk
in discussing how some growers go about making some money.

You must understand, in case you're not a grower yourself,
that the one way for growers to make any real money is to produce
preferably slightly less, but certainly no more of a crop
than the public will buy before the next crop becomes available.
How to do this in a field where man proposes and God disposes
is quite a problem. But since money is involved, it's no surprise
that man has figured out at least three ways to turn the trick.

One now tradition-honored way is to be a grower of the right
product—say corn or wheat or peanuts—and then not grow it.
You tell Uncle Sam you're not going to plant whatever-it-is,
and pretty soon one of his nephews brings around a fat check.
It's nice work if you can get it—and want it.

Another way to maybe not get rich but at least not go broke
is to grow some fruit (Ex.: California cantaloupes or peaches)
under a pre-agreed-on program which, in cases where Nature
has seen fit to be too generous, forces every such grower
to destroy (green drop) part of the crop before it matures.

A third way is to let Nature play Lady Bountiful and deliver
as big a crop as she desires, then harvest every last ton
but put the unwanted tonnage up on a back shelf someplace,
out of reach of the market, but available anytime it's needed.

The growers and vintners of California's Central Valley
have been following the third plan via the Grape Crush Order,
and how this has worked out is a matter of personal opinion.
You could guess, though, that while this setaside deal has helped,
it has fallen somewhat short of being completely satisfactory.
So it's now proposed to add the green drop principle
as a voluntary step for the growers, aided and abetted by a
mandatory surplus-destroying setup for the vintners.

How this will all pan out, assuming the growers okay the plan,
I can't anticipate. But feeling that the grower has every right
to fight for a reasonable return on his investment and labor,
I'm certain that, if this proposed path doesn't lead anywhere,
another road will be sought out and trod. For if history,
and particularly the history of economics, teaches us anything,
it teaches us that love (of money) will always find a way.

FEBRUARY, 1963

MIRACLE GAS

Carbon dioxide is a miracle gas.
Put it in a container under pressure and you can use it
in your place of business as a standby fire extinguisher.
Bring it down to extremely low temperature
and you have that very practical product known as "dry ice."
Force it into mixtures of water, sugar and flavorings
and it gives you the familiar bite of the soft drink.
Lay it as a blanket over your aging wine in a cask or tank
and it protects the wine from damaging contact with air.
Let it be created through fermentation in a bottle of your wine
and—presto!—the wine becomes Champagne.

Where does this precious yet inexpensive gas come from?
Its sources are almost as miraculously varied as its uses.
Manufacturing firms produce it by means of combustion
(burning natural gas, fuel oil and limestone is one way),
yeasts produce it through enzymatic action
(turning sugar into equal parts of alcohol and carbon dioxide)
—and man produces it simply by breathing (though no one
has yet been able to turn this to commercial advantage).

Of the many uses to which carbon dioxide is put,
that of transforming a still wine into champagne
is at once its most dramatic and, in the eyes of the
wine consuming public, certainly its most romantic aspect.
For this, the entire wine industry can be grateful,
since the almost universal acceptance of Champagne
as a beverage of romance has brought to that industry
a substantial plus in image and stature it might not have
if there were no wine like Champagne.

This brings us to the miracle of consumption gains
made by U. S. Champagne during the past quarter century.
From a yearly consumption mark of 400,000 gallons in 1937,
sales have zoomed to more than 4 million gallons in 1962,
which is about as far away from standing still as you can get,
and even farther away from the sales of some still wines.

Since it is the carbon dioxide that sets Champagne apart
from still wine, the Champagne producers have reason
to be grateful for the existence of this versatile gas.
So has our government. For what it sees in carbon dioxide
is a gas that possesses the wonderful capacity to transform
a 17 cent taxed wine into a $2.40 or $3.40 taxed wine.

Could anything possibly be more miraculous than that?

JUNE, 1963

PRESSURE

RECENTLY, I received an article from an industry member
with an appended note in his own handwriting challenging me:
"Do you have the *guts* to print this?"

The article did not appear in print in *Wines & Vines*.
My reasons for refusing to publish the piece are not grist
for today's editorial mill. What is, though, is the subtle
pressure applied by the author in his appeal to my courage.

An editor is subject to all sorts of pressures on editorial
matters, few of them subtle. Such pressures can come
from the powers-that-be within the publication itself,
or from persons of prominence in the field the magazine serves,
or from advertisers or their advertising agencies.

Such pressures can interfere—if the editor lets them—
with his primary job of putting together a publication
that will be of greatest value to the magazine's subscribers;
and without desiring to get Pollyanna-ish about it,
an editor who gives in to these pressures is not doing his job.

What brings this to my attention today has, fortunately,
nothing to do directly with my particular publication
but concerns a sister alcoholic beverage magazine, *Spirits*.

Recently, *Spirits* printed some comments which were interpreted
by a big distillery or its agency to be unfavorable to it.
As a direct result, all advertising from that distillery
was cancelled—and cancelled not only in *Spirits*
but also in retailer magazines from the same publisher.

Since it is advertising that breathes economic life
into any publication, such a curtailment is, in essence,
the brutal application of the most forceful possible pressure
to bring an editor "in line," and it chills me to consider
how blatantly the advertiser's action proclaimed
to the *Spirits* management, "You must please us, or else!"

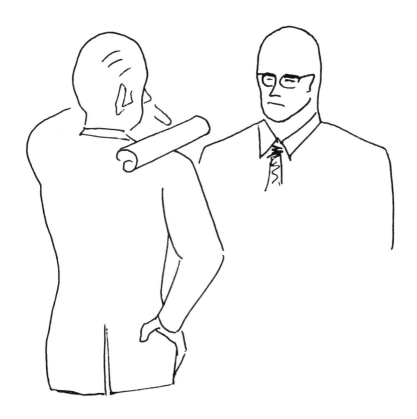

I believe any industry can well take pride
in a publication which dares to speak its editorial mind,
and I feel it is to the advantage of any industry's members
to have such a publication circulating among them.
I thus consider the distiller as being decidedly fortunate
to have, in *Spirits,* an outspoken industry medium.

For my part, I can only lend *Spirits* my moral support,
recognizing that this helps pay no publishing bills.

And I can only hope that, if *Wines & Vines* is ever faced
with the need for deciding between principle and principal,
I too will have the editorial guts to choose the former.

JULY, 1963

61

ITSY-BITSY BREAK

I was working on the San Francisco Stock Exchange
that "Black Thursday" in 1929 when the market broke
to make paupers of many on-paper millionaires
and I was still there through the depression years
when you could easily have picked up a 1000-to-1 bet
that the Dow Jones industrial average (down to 41)
would never again come near its former high of 386.
Today, the Dow Jones average stands at 702.

This brings me to the theme of this editorial
which is that what goes down must (or can) come up.

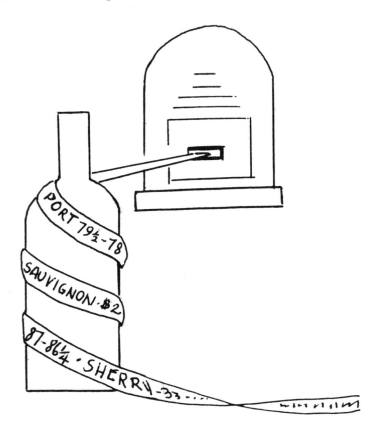

When statistics showed wine sales in calendar 1962
to be less than those in 1961, there were to be seen,
in some directions, the same signs of worry and even panic
that were visible after the 1929 stock market break.
Purse strings were tightened and horns were pulled in;
budgets were cut and promotional efforts were curtailed.
It seemed there was little or no confidence
in the come-back strength of the vintner's products.

The first six months of 1963 has given the lie
to the voices of doom raised such a short time back.
Business has been good, even "hot."
Carlot shipments from California wineries are far ahead
of the comparable totals for the previous year,
and this goes for both tank and packaged goods carlots.

Moreover—and don't ask me how this can happen
in view of the setback of calendar 1962—the recently
ended fiscal year (for which the statistics should come out
towards the end of this month) will almost surely show
that wine sales not only topped those of the previous
fiscal year, but in doing so set a new consumption high
(for the 11th fiscal year in a row).

I realize that, record or not, this doesn't mean
that every individual winery is participating in the rise,
any more than all stocks go up when the averages do.
(My shares, for example, act as if they believe Dow Jones
were spelled Down, Jones.) But surely, whether your books
reflect the change or not, it's important for you to recognize
that the current facts indicate the market for wine is *not*
falling off drastically, that indeed it holds promise
of going higher and higher—and that the real wonder of it
is how I (and maybe even you) saw everything so black
because of an itsy-bitsy setback in sales in 1962.

AUGUST, 1963

CORPUS DELICTI

With the Grape Crush Order dead—it *is* dead, isn't it?—
this appears to be the proper time for a wake
and a short funeral oration. But whether the wake
calls for gaiety ("I'm glad the rascal's gone")
or for tears ("How will we ever get along without him?")
is something that is hard to decide.

When the Grape Crush Order was first proposed,
I was willing to wager that it would never see life
(and thereby lost a chance to make a minor sort of killing
through the purchase of low-priced bulk dessert wine).

But within a month or so, there was a definite change
in the atmosphere, due to support—often grudgingly won—
from this group and that, this grower and the other,
but especially due to the bulldoggedness of a single man
who refused to believe the impossible couldn't be done.

Sox Setrakian was both father and mother to the Crush Order
and will be the chief mourner at its burial June 30, 1964.
(Say it again—you're *sure* it's dead?)

To hear others tell it, Setrakian brought a Frankenstein
into the world—and only by virtue of the *coup de grace*
delivered by the growers at the recent referendum
was the industry delivered from destruction by the very thing
which was supposed to save it.

Without holding a brief for Setrakian (who can do all right
in his own defense), I just can't buy making a scapegoat
of the initiator of this self-help program, no matter how soured
those complaining might be about the program's results.

After all, it was the growers who voted the Crush Order in,
and it was the growers who then voted it out—this time,
certainly, without any assistance from Setrakian.

Now the growers are "free" of the setaside provisions
of the Grape Crush Order. Yet is doesn't take an economist
to judge that 1963, with its record California grape crop,
is considerably less than likely to turn out to be
a get-rich-quick year for Central Valley grape growers.

Does this mean there's a chance for the Crush Order to rise,
like Lazarus, from the dead? Do you believe in miracles?

I don't either but, nearsighted as I am, don't I observe
some tremors in the central figure at this wake?
(Hey, Sox! Is the corpus *really* delicti?)*

SEPTEMBER, 1963

*P.S.: *It was.*

DIRTY WORD

The dirty word in the world of wine is *alcohol.*
Wine contains alcohol, and while there may be a hundred
or a thousand different reasons for buying wine,
its alcohol content is unquestionably one of them.

You can point out that the buyer of table wines
isn't primarily concerned with the alcohol in the wines.
And you can point out, too, that these are the wines
which have made the most impressive gains in recent years,
indicating that alcohol content isn't such a much.

But the fact of the matter is that, here in the U. S.,
the greatest volume of wine consumption is still
in aperitif and dessert wines, both of which have an
alcohol content that is in part responsible for their sales.

Sure, with these wines as with table wines, there are some,
perhaps many, who don't buy them simply for their alcohol.
But there are also some, and again perhaps many,
who buy these wines only *because* they contain alcohol.

Is this shameful? You would think so, noting how carefully
the industry avoids using the dirty word in public utterances.
Yet the sale of alcoholic beverages is legal,
the judicious use of such beverages is medically approved,
and the moderate consumption of alcohol
is known to relieve stress and improve human relations.

Maybe the vintner's problem lies in the words, "judicious"
and "moderate." A percentage of wine is known to be
injudiciously and immoderately consumed by down-and-outers,
who buy the wine mainly for its alcoholic content.

Yet these same down-and-outers also immoderately consume
whiskey and gin and rum, and the distillers don't seem to feel
that this—or the fact that almost everybody who buys spirits
does so *mainly* for its alcohol content—hurts their image
or their products. It may well be that the vintners
are "running scared" without reason.

I don't intend to imply here that the wineries
should deliberately go out and boast about the alcohol content
of their products (they couldn't legally, anyway),
but simply to suggest they should not publicly run away
from acknowledging that one of wine's major attractions
is the fact it contains a moderate amount of alcohol.

There! I've said the dirty word over and over again.
Should I wash my mouth out with soap?

NOVEMBER, 1963

NO

There's this Bart Browne, see, who's a columnist in "Bev" (successor to "Spirits" magazine) and who, as far as I know, has never edited a consumer magazine. Yet in a recent column he made so bold as to tell the editors of such magazines what to put—and more particularly what *not* to put— in their pages, and this is what I want to talk about.

You see, what this Bart Browne wants *not* to have the editors offer their readers are any more stories about wine. "The wine boys," he says, "are running off with the free space!"

The vintners, says this Bart Browne, have too many PR men working too hard. They are hoodwinking the innocent editors into using stuff which pushes the products of their "clients" while leaving spirits—whose producers buy so much more ad space—out in the editorial cold. You hear, editors?

I didn't know editors were supposed to be concerned with ads. I always believed editors selected articles primarily to catch and hold their readers' attention—as articles about wine, with its romance, have proved they can do. Do you suppose this Bart Browne really thinks that, if the editors suddenly decided on his say-so not to publish any more wine stories, they would then, as he advocates, substitute articles on other alcoholic beverages?

What of continuing interest would there be to present? The growing of grain to make into whiskey? The workings of a still to turn molasses into rum? The blending of neutral alcohol with water to make vodka? What does any one of these products offer as an editorial subject? Where is its romance, its color, its mystery? How many repetitive articles before it has been explored to the point of boredom?

Now, for contrast, take red table wine. There are forty, fifty, perhaps 100 *different* red tables wines, known by different names, made from different grapes in different districts of different countries—each individual, each varying from the others in color, flavor, bouquet, and even varying from itself as it matures year after year. This is something of what there is to write about in wine, and this is just red table wine!

You see why I rate this Bart Browne's comments as illogical, and why I wonder how these comments could appear in a magazine which proclaims it is "Devoted to the Liquor, Wine and Beer Industries." *Devoted* to the wine industry? Come now, who's kidding whom?

DECEMBER, 1963

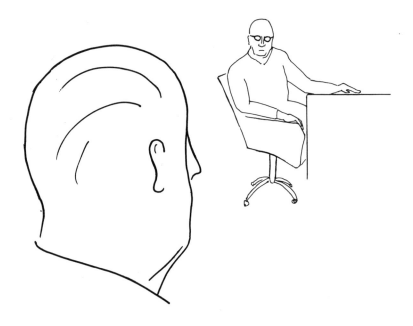

FLATTERING

Sometimes, an editor is the last to know,
but a number of readers have told me that the November article
comparing 1952 and 1962 wine sales on a state by state basis
was—and I quote—disturbing, disquieting, depressing.
I don't know whether to say, "I'm sorry" or "Good!"

I didn't set out to disturb, only to present some facts.
If the facts indicate to some industry individuals
that past sales gains have been something less than adequate
and that the consumer base has not been sufficiently broadened,
then these people have a right to feel disturbed.

Actually, the over-all picture is not too bad;
sales of 168 million gallons in 1962 were substantially ahead
of the 137 million gallons sold in 1952. What *is* depressing,
is that, in too many states, the populace seems able
to take wine or leave it alone without any sense of loss.

It has been suggested to me not to let the industry
"sweep the wine consumption article under the carpet,"
and it has been told me that it is up to me
"to inspire thought, examination and the development
of a program for industry growth and prosperity."
Well, I'm all for it, but will someone please tell me how?

Should I propose to the industry that it become more aggressive?
That it jump into a big-time ad program involving $10 million?
That it embark on still-stronger public relations projects?
That it accelerate the educational job it's doing?

What would be new about these suggestions?
They've appeared in this magazine many times in the past,
sometimes over my own signature for what that's worth,
sometimes under the by-lines of respected industry figures.
Have you noticed anyone rushing to get the job done?

Though it's true that the industry has never embarked
on what could be called a *total* promotional effort,
there are certain practical matters to be taken into account
before proposing such a program. It becomes, in the end,
a question not only of desire and/or method, but of cold cash.
You can't say, "Let's get the job done regardless of cost!"
because this could be sheer economic idiocy.

While I firmly believe additional promotional funds
could be spent to the considerable advantage of the industry,
and while I'd be the first to applaud such a step,
I doubt very much that all that's needed to get things going
are a few well chosen words from me. It is nevertheless
flattering that anyone—anyone!—should think so.

JANUARY, 1964

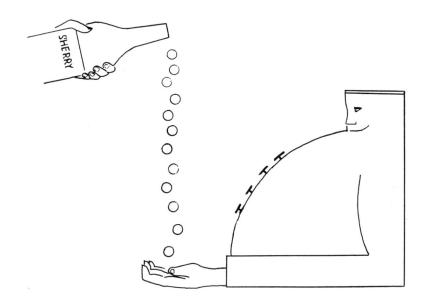

PROFIT

If I were a restaurant-bar owner and wanted to make *money,*
I'd sure go all out to sell sherry as an aperitif.

I decided this only the other day, after lunching with friends.
Waiting at the restaurant bar for a table, three of us ordered
California sherry. It turned out that the place carried
only one California brand, this in the popular price category.
From a half-full bottle, the bartender poured maybe 1½ oz. into
each of three tiny glasses and rang up the charge: $1.50.

Well, this wasn't cheap, yet not overwhelmingly costly.
As I paid the amount, though, it came to me suddenly
that the bar owner wasn't losing any money on this sale,
and when I got back to the office, I took out the price book
and started figuring just how much he wasn't losing.
Here's what I came up with.

The bar owner had paid $6.60 for a case of this sherry (less, if he had taken advantage of the quantity discount). So, if he had poured 1½ oz. into each glass—a generous estimate of what we got—each pouring had cost him some 3½ cents. His charge of 50 cents thus provided him with a gross return of 1500%—somewhat better than the usual bank rates.

Looking at it another way, by the sale of a mere 1½ oz. of wine, the bar owner had recovered almost the full cost of his Fifth. From still another angle: before the last drop is poured from the first bottle in a case, the bar owner will have got back well above the cost of the entire case. And a final angle: by investing a mere $6.60, the bar owner bought for himself a potential gross return of $102.80. Wow! I thought. I wonder if bar owners know about this?

Don't think this kind of return resulted only because this particular bar owner purchased a popular priced sherry. If he'd had a premium priced U. S. sherry, he'd probably have upped his charge to 60 cents; and for the still more costly foreign sherries, he would likely have gone to 75 cents. None of these price levels would show a loss.

Consider, too, that all this nice sherry profit would come without the need of any muss or fuss on the bartender's part; he'd open the bottle and pour; that's all it would take.

Yes, sir, if I were a restaurant-bar owner, I'd not only give sherry a big push every chance I got, but I'd pour generous 2 oz. or even 2½ oz. servings. I'm no hog; a gross profit of 1000% would satisfy me fine.

MARCH, 1964

TROUBLES

You think *you* have troubles?
Ask the man next to you at the bar about his.
Or listen to a merchandiser in a field other than yours.
Or even—if you dare—ask your wife.
Everybody, you'll find, has troubles.
Why should the wine industry be different?

Today's troubles in the wine industry
include some problems which are old and some which are new.
Among the new are the proposed twin Marketing Orders
that would place certain limitations on winery operations.
These mean trouble because some vintners are for them
and some are against them, and even a Solomon
couldn't find a solution which would please both sides.

Then there's the trouble—with California vintners, anyway—
of their spending themselves practically busted on their
Wine Advisory Board educational and promotional efforts.
The out-go is bigger than the in-come; and with everything
(except maybe wine) costing more and more each year,
something obviously has got to be done. Only what?

And you must admit there's at least the smell of trouble
in upcoming negotiations with the winery workers' union,
for if there is anything certain in such negotiations,
it is that the result will not be lower labor costs.

Then there's the problem of trying to outguess Nature.
Like, will there be another of those too-big crops?
Or will the Thompson Seedless harvest actually be light?
Or what kind of a comeback will the badly frosted vines
of the North Coast area make? Guess right and you're money ahead.
Guess wrong . . .

There's also the long continuing worry about what to do
to get dessert wine sales going in the right direction.
And trying to decide if Flavored wines have had it
or are just pausing before again leaping ahead dramatically.
And figuring out how to halt the long downward slide
in import duties on wines and brandies.
And what to do to keep the various state legislatures
from trying to squeeze more money out of the wine industry
than the wine industry squeezes out of the grapes.

Troubles? Yes, the wine industry and the vintners
have their full share. Just like everybody.
Me? Any time you've got a couple of hours to spare . . .

MAY, 1964

CUSTOMER'S DOLLAR

Even in this best of all merchandising worlds,
you find the average man reluctant to let go of his money.
There are, nevertheless, a number of ways of overcoming
this reluctance. You can do it, to cite one example,
by use of a loaded pistol, if you happen to be a robber.
Or you can do it simply by telling the man you want your share,
if you happen to be the Director of Internal Revenue.
But if, like most, you're just a business man,
about the only legitimate way you can get the reluctant spender
to really put out, is to persuade him that what you offer him
is worth more to him than a specified amount of his cash.

Here you have the secret of successful merchandising.
But you have the secret only if you understand it.
For the formula of successful merchandising is not so much
to be found in the worth of the product you offer the man,
as it is in your capacity to *persuade him to recognize that worth.*

Obviously, this calls for some sort of communication
between you and the man whose dollars you hope to garner.
Assuming that your business is big enough to make it impossible
for you to talk in person with each potential customer,
you've got to use some other means to get your story across.
You're faced, in other words, with the need for using advertising
or public relations, or both, to reach your man.

How successful this necessary effort becomes depends
on how correctly you (or your ad or PR agency) judges what it is
that you have to sell, and how best to make the potential customer
(who is carrying your dollars around in his pocket)
feel that, in buying from you, he's getting more than he's giving.

What story will do the most for you? The best quality theme?
The lowest price? The greatest taste pleasure? The snob symbol?
The buy American pitch? There are all sorts of sales stories.
If you pick the right one, or the right combination,
and if your product can live up to the claims you make for it
(which means don't use superlatives unless your product
is worth them), you're on the way to having it made.

Sounds mighty easy, doesn't it? But of course it isn't,
or every businessman would quickly become a millionaire.
No, it's not at all easy. But it *is* necessary,
and if you don't do it, your company will surely suffer,
and that consumer dollar you think of as being properly yours,
will end up with the man who *did* talk to his customers.

JUNE, 1964

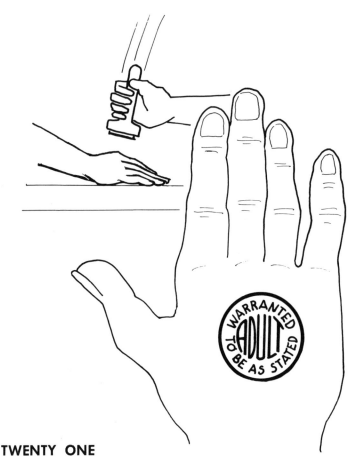

TWENTY ONE

One of the foibles under which we live
is that the government can, in its infinite wisdom,
select the proper age at which a child becomes an adult,
opening the path for the boy-turned-man to drive a car,
join the service, vote, or even drink alcoholic beverages.

Granting that *somebody* has to make this sort of decision,
any parent will understand the difficulty in recognizing
the actual arrival of adulthood in a particular offspring,
and will bear witness that one child is more mature at sixteen
than another is at twenty. So the government's job isn't easy.

This makes it understandable that a youngster of 14
is permitted to drive a car in one state but in another state
must wait until he's sixteen, and that an eighteen-year-old
is permitted to imbibe in one state but must wait until he's 21
to buy an alcoholic beverage legally in another.

What brings this to mind at the moment is that
a California legislator, aroused at the number of under-21
youngsters who are passing themselves off as being of legal
drinking age, has advocated lowering that age to 18.

If the eighteen, nineteen and twenty year olds are going
to drink—and they are, he says—it's better to make it
legal for them to do so, than to force them to go through
the subterfuge of claiming 21-year-old "maturity."

Well, everybody is entitled to his opinion, even an editor,
and mine is that dropping the 21 year age limitation to 18
would resolve absolutely nothing.

I grant that, where 21 is the legal drinking age,
a number of youngsters in the 18-to-20 bracket
will manage to pass themselves off successfully as being 21.
Anybody who believes this can be stopped by law is dreaming.

But once you set the age limit at 18, what will happen?
It is then the sixteen and seventeen year olds who will,
in their rush to be recognized as "adults," try to pass
themselves off as being of legal drinking age.
And don't think some of them won't get by with it.

It may be that those states which have an 18 year minimum
(New York, for example) don't find this to be a problem;
and it may be that, in my advancing years, I'm becoming
an old fogie. But since, things being what they are,
some minimum drinking age appears to be needed,
I can't see what's wrong with 21.

AUGUST, 1964

CRAZY, MAN

It was maybe some fifteen or more years ago,
when Californians were buying 2½ bottles of dessert wine
to every bottle of table wine they purchased,
that I predicted—"Crazy," some said—that the time would come
when table wines would outsell desserts in that state.

Today, table wine sales in California are so far ahead
of dessert wine volume, it's no contest anymore.
Now, I'm beginning to believe that what Californians did,
many other states are on the verge of doing.

I didn't come to that conclusion by tossing a coin,
or by star gazing, or even by looking in a crystal ball.
I simply looked at the record.

What I saw was that (1) Sales of California table wines
in California through the first seven months of this year
were making a nice (9%) advance over that of record 1963,
(2) Shipments of California table wines to OTHER states
(where dessert wines still outsell table wines 2½ to 1)
were advancing at a *much faster (15.51%) pace.*

You may say—and you'd probably be right—that this
is a pretty weak basis on which to make such a prediction.
But the proper time to make any kind of prediction
(at least if you want to be able to say "I told you so!"),
is when most others think you're out of your head.

Before we go any further into this matter of lunacy, though,
let me check you on your own attitudes towards the future
of wine in this country, to see where you differ from me.

If you're like most industry people I've talked to,
you feel confident wine volume is going to move ahead. Right?
Yet you hold out little hope that the dessert wines
will contribute any substantial gains. Right?
You therefore believe that whatever sales gains are made
will be made mainly in table wines, with maybe an assist
from Champagne and a tiny push from Vermouth. Right?
And you *must* believe that people living outside of California
are basically the same as the residents of that state
(most of whom came from somewhere else, anyway). Right?

Right! In essence, then, you've agreed with me completely.
So while I don't deny the possibility that I must be crazy
to believe table wine sales will move up dramatically
in states outside of California, I have one comforting thought
—If I *am* crazy, I have lots of company.

OCTOBER, 1964

MIGHTIER

The pen is mightier than the sword.
Author Bulwer Lytton coined this adage about a century ago,
and for all I know, may have invented it simply because
he was a good man with a pen and a lousy swordsman.
But the idea he put into words was sound.

The proof is to be found in a remarkable document
which appeared in mid-1964. This was a doctoral thesis
dealing with the artificial protection extended Washington
wine growers by that northwestern state's legislature.
In cold print, the thesis clearly showed the extreme bias
with which the Washington solons had acted to protect
their state's wines against the kind of competition
every other product sold in Washington faces.

This document must have been a shock to those who read it.
But the public is not given to reading doctoral theses,
and it took another bit of penmanship to win public attention.

This was an article published in *Seattle* magazine last month.
It depicted the difficulty, in some cases the near impossibility,
of a Washington state resident exercising a free choice
in the selection of a wine other than one made in Washington.
This article kicked up quite a public fuss.

So? So a group of Washington citizens formed the Consumers'
Protective Council, one of whose specific goals is to force
repeal of the discriminatory taxes and selling conditions
faced by non-Washington wine.

This is no ordinary anti-anti group. It has the backing
of a dozen recognized business and labor organizations,
and it is believed to have the voice to make itself heard.
It will ask the legislature to grant Washington residents
"equal rights" with citizens of Open States to buy wines
of their choice at reasonable prices in regular retail outlets.

You may recall that, a few years back, the state of California
tried to achieve this same end for the people of Washington
by charging the latter state with unconstitutional restraint
of trade through its discriminatory taxes against California wines.

This, in a way, was the "sword" approach to the problem.
It failed when the U. S. Supreme Court ruled it didn't want
to referee this inter-state duel. Now, the entire matter
has become an internal Washington affair, with action promised.
So where the sword failed, the pen looks likely to succeed.

Makes a man who lives by the pen feel good.

NOVEMBER, 1964

NUMBERS

LIKE you, I'm getting more and more to be known by numbers.
To the people who run the nation's Social Security program,
for example, I'm not a name at all; I'm simply 558-01-3106.
To the local phone company, I'm neither name nor address;
I'm 415-392-1146. As for the Post Office, to it I'm merely one
of some thousands who live in that specific part of the country
designated as 94105 (and pretty soon, if you don't use this code,
I won't get your letter, whether or not you spell my name right).
Even at the San Francisco Press Club, to which I've belonged
for some three decades, if I don't sign 1569 on the chits,
the club personnel insist—horrors!—on cash.

This editorial concentration on numbers is merely the result
of having sat in as a guest at a recent dinner meeting
of the San Francisco chapter of the Society of Bacchus,
where the talk got around to still another type of number
with which certain people concern themselves—vintage dates.

The members of the Society of Bacchus, I think you should know,
are persons concerned with the serving of food and drink
to patrons of the swankier restaurants and hotel dining rooms.
To a man, at the dinner which I attended, the Society members
expressed themselves as being at least 100% in favor
of having vintage dates on as many bottles as possible.

As one of them pointed out, with a vintage date on the bottle,
he could ask and get at least an extra dollar for the wine,
and what better argument could there be to a man
who lives and dies by the numbers on the cash register?

When I suggested that some competent people believe every year
can be rated as a vintage year in California, I was told,
"Then there should be no problem in using vintage dates,"
and I began to suspect I had put my foot in it.

I was sure of it when one of the guests added, "Nonsense!
California wine quality definitely varies from year to year."
Since he had been the Society's selection as Mr. Gourmet 1964,
and I hadn't been selected even Mr. Maybe of any year,
I felt it was time for me to shut up—which, hard as it may be
for those of you who know me to believe, I promptly did.

I came away from that dinner very well fed indeed,
but with an increasing worry that there were too many people
who seemed not only to desire, but actually to need numbers
to get through life. So, leaving you with that sad thought,
this is 0067-829-002—that's me at the bank—signing off.

JANUARY, 1965

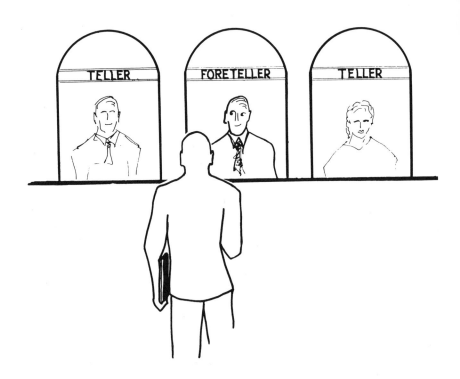

WRONG

There's a lot to be said for being the biggest anything
(except possibly the biggest fool), and there's therefore a lot
to be said for the Bank of America, the world's biggest bank.
Yet I'm going to limit myself to a comparatively few words.

In a recent evaluation of the wine industry's future, the Bank
(the capital "B" honors the capital worth of this institution),
predicted that U. S. sales of table wine would top dessert wine
sales in the next five to eight years—and if that was you
who said "Wow!" it's understandable.

I respect the Bank (it's a partner with me in a home I "own").
But I feel that the Bank's prediction is super-super-optimistic,
and before you table wine producers raise your hopes too high,
I feel it's my editorial duty to show you why the Bank is wrong.

First, remember that table wine is still an "odd ball" beverage
to the great majority of U. S. residents. It's for foreigners,
and beatniks, and strange beings who call themselves connoisseurs.
This attitude is not likely to change in the near future.

Second, table wine is low in alcohol, and while this may have
some appeal to some people, how far do you suppose you can get
with low alcohol in a nation that goes for 20-to-1 martinis?

Third—and this is the clincher—the gap between table wine
and dessert wine sales is just too big to close in five to eight years.
Look. In 1963 (last year for which there are complete figures),
there were 64 million gallons of table wine sold in the U. S.
That same year, dessert wine sales totaled 85 million gallons.
That's a 21 million gallon gap. Close this in five to eight years?
I hate to throw cold water on such a nice dream, but . . .

Let's apply cold statistics to the problem. Let's check what
table wines have gained over desserts in, say, the past six years,
let's project these findings six years into the future;
then let's see what is *really* likely to happen.

In 1957, table wine sales hit 45 million gals. (a then record),
while desserts sold 94.6 million gals. This is a difference
of 49.6 million gals. Right? Six years later, in 1963,
the comparable figures still showed a gap of 21 million gals.
Now, think. If it took six years to close a 49.6 million gallon
gap to 21 million gallons, then you can readily see that . . .

Wait a minute. I must have made an error adding or subtracting
or something. Let me check it again. In 1957, table wine sales
were 45 million gallons. In 1963, table wine sales . . . H-m-m?

You want to know something? Table wine sales in the U. S.
will top dessert wine sales within the next *four* years.

I just knew the Bank was wrong.*

*P.S.: So was I. Table wine did it in three years.

THIS KIND

I don't know about you, but I'm not a cigaret smoker.
Nor do I own shares in any firm that manufactures cigarets.
So it was only natural for me to kind of slide over the news
that the Federal Trade Commission had recently ruled that,
come mid-year, all cigaret packages must carry a statement
on the label saying that the contents are hazardous to health
and may cause death. Obviously, this had nothing to do
either with me or with wine.

Which just goes to show how little I'm up on things.
Apparently, during the time the FTC was considering what to do
about cigarets, somebody was pushing the idea that,
if cigarets were to be forced to carry a health warning,
why not alcoholic beverages?

Who was doing the pushing, I don't know. But I'm happy to say that the Federal Trade Commission pushed right back. Said the FTC, in its own, more moderate words, "Nuts."

Well, sir! If you've been around as long as I have, you'll maybe understand how unusual it is for an august governmental body to jump to the defense of alcoholic beverages. Most times, when such beverages come up for consideration by this or that governmental arm, it is for the purpose of imposing stricter-than-ever-before regulations, or extracting higher-than-ever-before taxes.

The industry is used to this and to combatting such efforts. As for myself, sitting at the editorial desk, such actions provide me with a chance to do some real ranting and raving (for it's always easier to be against something than for it).

But these people on the Federal Trade Commission! Instead of doing something nasty, something I can get my vituperative teeth into—why, these men spoke right up and said a number of nice things about alcoholic beverages.

Like noting that alcohol in moderation is often prescribed by doctors. And that consuming alcoholic beverages is not nearly as habit forming as cigaret smoking. And that the alcoholic beverage people, by self-regulation, have established operational codes rated as praiseworthy.

What can even the nastiest editor write about such people? That they are reasoning, mature beings who have recognized that wine, beer, whiskey, Scotch, gin, vodka, etc., all have a proper place in this world? What kind of an aggressive, dynamic industry editorial would that make?

Come to think of it, this kind. Sorry.

MARCH, 1965

89

WHO, ME?

A funny thing happened to me on my way to the future
—the American Society of Enologists selected me
to receive its Merit Award for 1965. Yes, me.

To say I'm pleased and flattered would hardly do justice
to my feelings. Anybody likes to be singled out for an honor,
and I am taking this public way of serving notice
on the members of the American Society of Enologists
that I am accepting the award proffered me.

I don't suppose the ASE was worried about my not accepting;
but after all, writers like Bernard Shaw and more recently Sartre
have turned down the Nobel prize, so I thought I'd mention
my acceptance in case there was any doubt anywhere.

That I do so shouldn't come as a surprise to anyone.
As I am sure all readers must be aware by now,
it takes a certain amount of ego to sit at a typewriter
and offer presumably sage advice to people who have proved
in their own separate ways to be smarter than you are.
Such an ego is part of an editor's stock in trade.

This being the case, I not only wouldn't think
of turning down the Award, but I would fight tooth and nail
for it should the ASE suddenly find out next week
that it was all a matter of mistaken identity,
and that the Award should have really gone to a Marcus
who had forced through a law specifying that the enologist
must be the most highly paid person in a winery.

Now, if I can diverge just a bit from the main topic,
let me say that one of the problems of being an editor
and talking to people on a one-way line via the printed word
is that, when you write something worth a verbal pat
(and if you write enough, you're *bound* to say something good
from time to time), you hardly ever hear from the readers.
But when you say something not so good—well, let it pass.

So I'll confess I'm looking forward with some excitement
to the annual banquet of the American Society of Enologists,
to be held at the Sacramento Inn the evening of June 26.

Some time during that evening, in the normal sequence of events,
an ASE member will get up and say a number of nice things
about me right out loud (sort of justifying their selection).
I can assure that person, whoever he may turn out to be,
that no matter how long his talk (and I don't want him to rush)
he'll have at least one avid listener—me.

APRIL, 1965

WEAPON

I've gotten into a bad habit.
Every time I go out to dinner, I peer at other tables
to see how many dining patrons are drinking wine.
My wife says it's rude of me, but all I'm doing
is what show people call counting the house.

Since I live in San Francisco, where table wine consumption
is probably the highest per capita of all U. S. cities,
I must admit that the count is usually quite satisfactory,
with from 15% to 40% of the tables boasting a bottle of wine.

Those in the wine trade in France would probably be appalled
at what they would call so few wine drinkers, and even more
appalled at my satisfaction in this direction.

Let these French tradesmen be appalled.
I know something they don't know—that the drinking of wine
is still a new and even a strange concept to most of those
I see in restaurants. Even in "drinkingest" San Francisco.

There are all kinds of reasons put forward as to why
the restaurants of San Francisco do such good wine business,
as compared with most other metropolitan U. S. centers.

Some say it is the nearness of the California wineries,
which tends to make people more conscious of wine.
Others believe it is because of the Latin heritage
of so high a percentage of the population.
A third group holds that the basic reason is simply that
most S. F. restaurants price their wines at reasonable levels.
Still others offer the argument that the restaurateurs
in San Francisco actually do a promotional job on wine.

Any or all of these arguments may be right.
I subscribe in part to every one of them.
But I stand by my guns that one of the overlooked factors
in boosting the sale of wine in San Francisco
is my secret weapon—my habit of pointedly noting
which diners do and which do not have wine on the table
(thus presumably making those without wine uncomfortable).

Don't be surprised, then, next time you dine in San Francisco,
if you find a heavy-ish, bald man with horn rim glasses
staring rudely at the contents of your table.
Even though San Francisco abounds in heavy-ish bald men
with horn rim glasses who are rude, this is likely me.
So please don't get insulted. A wine magazine editor
has to do his job as he sees it.

MAY, 1965

BANQUET

I shouldn't bite the hand that feeds me, but I'm going to.
I'm going to sink my editorial teeth into the hand (or hands)
of the Board of Directors of the California State Fair,
who fed me gratis earlier this month.

The Board consists of a number of fine upright citizens
—successful businessmen, sophisticated in appearance,
pleasant conversationalists; all in all a wonderful group.
Only they sure don't know how to put on a banquet.

How do I know? From my experience the night of September 4.
That evening, at the invitation of the Fair's Board,
I was a guest at the directors' annual Press-Radio-TV Dinner.
I drove the ninety miles to Sacramento with happy anticipation;
first because I was to receive a gold medal at the banquet;
and second, because I *like* banquets.

Now, to me, a banquet isn't just a meal;
meals I can get at home or in a nearby restaurant.
A banquet is more. It is a group of people enjoying themselves;
it is an affair that has a constant ebb and flow of movement;
it is an occasion that pulses with excitement; it is a scene
that is particularly marked by the sound of multiple voices
on the constant rise. When a banquet gets to the point
where you can't hear yourself talk—*that's* a party.

Sad to relate, the State Fair banquet, a quasi-official affair
with Governor Pat Brown in attendance, was no such thing.
If there is an antonym for banquet, *that* is what it was.

The reason why is simple: no alcoholic beverages were served.
There were no pre-dinner drinks—and no wine on the table.
A WCTU member would have felt at home in the banquet hall.

I can take alcohol or leave it alone. I prefer to take it.
Particularly, I prefer to take it when I go to a party,
at which time I imbibe modestly. If I must go without
a pre-dinner drink, I'm willing. But without wine?

I can't speak for anybody else, but when I sit down to eat,
in my own home or at somebody else's house, in a restaurant
or at some big dining function, I can't conceive of thoroughly
enjoying my food and myself without wine at the table.
As for calling food without wine a banquet—Well!

So this is a reminder to Governor Brown, to the Fair Board,
and to anyone else who might be planning a banquet:
If you really *MEAN* it to be a banquet—
Put wine on the table!

SEPTEMBER, 1965

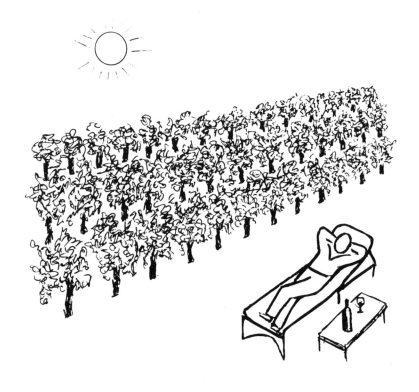

VINTNER

In the past couple of decades, literally dozens of men
have dropped into my office to ask my opinion of a bright idea
that has been in the back of their minds for a long time.
It is always the same idea—they want to embark
on wine growing as a pleasant way of life.

Some were well advanced in age, and it was their belief
that making wine would be a very happy and profitable way
of spending their retirement years. As for the younger ones,
it was their almost universal opinion that earning a living
as a vintner would be more "fun"—a popular word in describing
winemaking—than doing it on their present job.

I like to think I gave these visitors sage advice.
In the main, what I said amounted to: "Don't do it."
I said this in spite of being certain it would be good
for the image of the wine industry to have a greater number
of small operators making limited gallonages of wine.

Mere willingness is not enough to make a man a vintner.
What it takes, as I see it, is money, sales ability,
winemaking knowledge—and above all, what is called "guts."
I interpret guts as being a sort of psychological inability
to recognize when you're licked, thus giving you the chance
to win out over all sorts of handicaps.

Like you, I've watched a few newcomers make the grade.
But I've seen more fall by the wayside, and knowing the odds,
I'm reluctant to give a man with stars in his eyes
the impression that that's all he needs to make a success.

The mere fact that a man wants to make a dream come true
(which is how many visitors put it) by no means guarantees
that the dreamer will be able to face up to the reality.
Commercial winemaking, I warn my visitors, is a business,
with all the work, all the headaches, all the risks of business.

To tell the truth, I make it sound pretty tough.
And when I get through, many who came into the office
spouting about the romance and the beauty of making wine,
leave it certain they've had a narrow escape with disaster.

Since, by letting me dissuade them, they've proved
they haven't got what it takes, I feel reasonably certain
I've done the right thing by them. But do you know what?
While these men were listening to me, I was listening to them,
and on my retirement I'm determined to become a vintner
and enjoy that beautiful, romantic life they described so well.

NOVEMBER, 1965

97

NON-DRINKERS

You'd never guess it now, but I was once a non-imbiber.
This was in the 1930's, through the last years of prohibition
and the early years of Repeal; and since in those days,
I was going around with a pretty hard-drinking group,
I was probably the busiest non-drinker on the speakeasy circuit
(I had keys and cards to at least a dozen speakeasies).

Because most people I came in contact with in those days
knew I was a non-imbiber, I was rarely faced with the need
for turning down a proffered drink. But when such a need arose,
my pet phrase was, "No, thanks; I'm on the wagon."

This was not quite honest. Being "on the wagon" implied
that I was a drinker who had decided to lay off temporarily.
But it was difficult for me then, as it is difficult
for others now, to come right out and say, "I don't drink."

This is so because those who are imbibers—the majority—
seem to look on non-drinkers—the minority—as being
odd balls of some kind. The non-drinker gets this feeling
quite quickly, and embarks on a method of protecting himself
by turning down offered drinks with euphemistic remarks—
"Not just now, thanks" or "Maybe later."

The logical conclusion to draw from this particular pattern
of human behavior is that there is some sort of social stigma
attached to being a non-drinker.

While I am involved in an industry whose very existence
depends on the acceptance of moderate drinking as a normal way
of life (a philosophy to which I subscribe heartily),
I still cannot help but resent this sort of public attitude
—if, indeed, it exists.

I say "if" because there is a possibility,
perhaps even a probability, that the public in general
doesn't give a damn whether a particular man drinks or not.
This leads inevitably to a new conclusion—that the
non-drinker creates his own mental barrier to declaring
himself openly and without worry as a non-imbiber.

Recently, I met a man who turned down my offer of a drink
by remarking matter-of-factly, "No, thanks; I don't drink.
I'm an alcoholic." If one man can make such a statement
without seeming at all flustered or guilt laden,
then I feel that anyone with the minor social problem
of being a non-drinker should not fear to say so right out.

Non-drinkers of the world, arise!

DECEMBER, 1965

LAW BREAKER

I know something about you. You're a law breaker.

You're a law breaker because there are so many odd laws
that even the best-intentioned people break some unwittingly.
So I know you do. Just as I know I do.

Sometimes, I even break a law knowingly.
One that I break is the California law that tells me
I don't have the right to serve my own minor children
an alcoholic beverage, even within the confines of my own home.

If, like me, you're a Californian with minor children
(and especially if you're connected with the wine industry),
chances are that you're breaking this law right along with me.
And if you're a parent living in some other state,
I'll bet the law is just as strict for you as it is for me.

I have no objection to a law directed towards halting
the indiscriminate serving of alcoholic beverages to minors.
But to stop the judicious serving of, say, wine
to your own children within the confines of your own home?
This is not only silly, but there is plenty of evidence
that it stands in the way of temperate consumption.

Research on drinking seems to prove that, where wine consumption
is a casual entire-family matter within the home, the children
of the house grow up to be men and women with the same
sane attitude towards alcohol as that held by their parents.

This is an obvious plus for Society.
Yet Society tells the parent, "Stop! You can't do that!"

Look at what happens under the law to you, if you're a vintner
with a teenage son you're grooming to take over your job.
Naturally, you want your son to know how to judge wine.
But can you, in your winery or your home, legally give him
even a start towards tasting and evaluating wine?

No, sir, you cannot.

The baker can pass his knowledge on to his son from infancy;
So can the chef and the butcher and the dairyman.
But you teach your teenager the elements of wine judging?
The law is specific and definite: You may do no such thing.

It may be that, as a generally law abiding vintner,
you have let this law stop you from doing a proper job
in teaching your son the essentials of wine evaluation.
But if it has—well, then I don't know anything
about human beings or about vintners with offspring.

Gentlemen, welcome to the club of law breakers.

JANUARY, 1966

D — — — !

Nobody knows for sure, but it's generally presumed
that about one American adult out of five is a wine drinker.
How many of these statistical wine drinkers rate the term
only by grace of a glassful or two taken on rare "occasions,"
or by the fact that they put a drop or two of Vermouth
into what they call a martini, I wouldn't try to guess.

In my job, I'm naturally interested in those one-in-fives.
But to tell the truth, I'm really much more interested
in the other four who don't warrant the term wine drinker
even under the most liberal definition.

Being interested, and being an editor, I've become quite nosey
about these non-wine drinkers—even to the point
of asking maybe a couple of hundred of them blankly, "Why?"

As you might suspect, I have gotten all sorts of answers,
from the apologetic—"I'm sorry, but it never enters my mind"
—to the damning of wine for one reason or another.

Among those who damn wine are some, I've found, who do so
because wine contains alcohol and they're against alcohol.
Then there are those who damn wine because it contains alcohol
but not *enough* alcohol. In addition, there are a number
who damn wine because they consider it a snob beverage
—as well as others who damn it because it's not enough
of a snob beverage, it's that stuff the bums drink.

None of this disturbs me too much. What *does* bother me
is that the majority who tell me they don't drink wine
say it's because they—and I quote—"don't like the taste."

THE taste?

The concept always floors me.
There is *the* taste in bourbon, and *the* taste in scotch.
There is *the* taste in gin, and *the* taste in rum.
But how in the world can anyone say THE taste in wine?

The industry produces some 60 different wine types,
each type having its separate and unique characteristics
in terms of body, sweetness, color, astringency, and acidity;
each having an individuality that is expressedly its own.

How can anybody—mind you, anybody!—look at this array,
lump them all together in a single class like milk, and say
"I don't like the taste"? In my younger, more innocent days,
before I learned better, I would have sworn that this
was absolutely impossible. I would have sworn it.

Now, I just swear.

FEBRUARY, 1966

MAGIC

The U. S. public still believes in magic.
To be more exact, Dr. Michael Shenkman believes
the public believes in magic—the magic of words.

Dr. Shenkman proved this when he proposed, in a series of
of articles and letters published in medical journals,
that medical men throw out the evil word, "alcoholism,"
and substitute the good words, "Jellinek's disease."
A number of medics have indicated that they agree.

The word, "alcoholism," said the doctor, "is loaded with
moralistic undertones." These interfere with the acceptance
of this disease *as* a disease by the patient or by the family.
Tell patient and family, however, that they are dealing
with a case of Jellinek's disease—and presto!—you obtain
a completely different psychological approach to the problem;
a more objective consideration of the disease.

Such objectivity on the part of the patient, the doctor feels,
can be the first step towards controlling the disease.

If the objectivity extends to the family, so much the better.
If it extends to hospitals, better yet. "Few hospitals,"
says the doctor, "will accept alcoholics under the diagnosis
of alcoholism." But someone suffering from Jellinek's disease?

Don't take this to mean that the doctor feels the use
of a euphemism for alcoholism will really fool anyone.
Everyone concerned will know exactly what he's dealing with,
but as long as he doesn't see or hear the blunt word,
the negative psychological impact of the word will be lessened,
and in time possibly buried.

I admit it makes sense. But nevertheless, I'm a bit disturbed.
I'm disturbed to think that, in as adult a community
as I think the U. S. is, among the most sophisticated national
group that ever existed in the history of the world,
acknowledgement of the existence of a disease can be won
only by applying to it specifically selected words.

If words have this power (and they probably have),
then it appears to me that we are dealing with something
that edges on incantation, on magic. Say the right word
and your wish comes true, your unhappiness turns to happiness,
your illness goes away, your troubles vanish.

This is gross exaggeration on my part, of course.
But isn't this the root of the good doctor's proposal?
And isn't he likely right?

Abracadabra!

MARCH, 1966

DECISION

Whether it be in an office, on the football field,
or in a court of law, somebody has to have the final say.
In the United States as a whole, I guess the final say
is in the hands of the august U. S. Supreme Court.
Last month, this court ruled in essence that advertising
doesn't really raise the value of goods.

The point under consideration was whether the Borden Company
could wholesale its milk, packaged under others' private labels,
for less than it wholesales that milk under its own brand.
The court, seven to two, ruled that it could not,
and this decision warrants editorial attention here
because the concept could be applied to the wine industry,
where private labelling is certainly not unknown.

The Borden argument was that, even if the composition
of the milk was admittedly the same in both cases,
the company, by advertising its brand, had added a plus
in consumer value to the milk selling under the Borden label
that was not there under the non-advertised private brand.

The court said Nonsense, the advertising didn't change
the actual worth of the product to the consumer,
so the advertising really didn't add anything of value.

Who am I to argue with the U. S. Supreme Court?
Don't answer that.
But I can't help wondering if the court,
in making its decision in this precedent-setting case,
considered how much of an impact a purchaser's *belief*
that a particular brand is better than other brands,
has on his satisfaction in using or consuming that product.

Brand advertising is intended to bring about such a belief,
based on an actual or implied or imagined product difference.
Yet even when all brands of a product are exactly alike,
I hold that a man who is persuaded to believe Brand A is best
gets a psychological plus out of the use of this brand
which he does not get from using any other brand.

Consider the case of aspirin, which has an exact formulation
regardless of whose brand name is on the box. I have friends,
and I'll warrant that you have too, who insist that,
when they use Bayer aspirin (the most advertised and costliest
of all aspirin brands), their headaches go away faster.

Induced self-delusion? Possibly. Worth paying extra for?
Don't look at me. I'm not on the Supreme Court bench.

APRIL, 1966

BLIND

There are a substantial number of Americans
who consider American wine to be an arrant upstart,
a beverage trying to ape its betters, in much the same way
that a *nouveau riche* social climber tries to copy
the manner and pattern of living of those "above" him.
If you've been around wine any time at all,
you will have come across characters of this kind
with an almost depressing regularity.

As for me, maybe once, twice, or even three times a week,
depending on how unlucky I happen to be,
I find myself face to face with an individual
who holds this opinion of California or other U. S. wines.
The usual four letter word applied to such is "snob."

What irritates me about a snob of this kind
is not that he has an opinion contrary to mine—I'd be mad
at half the world half the time if that were the case—
but that he has so often settled on his fixed opinion
without giving the wines of this country a chance.

Occasionally, I suggest to such a biased person
that, perhaps for his own benefit, he should undertake
(on his own, and with no one to pressure him)
to blind test some of the foreign wines he admires
against some of the American wines I admire.

Actually, I am not too hopeful that even such a test
would persuade a wine-biased person that he could be wrong.
I've watched a number of tastings where foreign wines
were blind-paired with California wines of the same kind,
and I've marked the surprise which some of the tasters showed
when they found they had unknowingly given California wines
a higher standing than the comparative European wines.
Surprised, they most certainly were. But convinced?

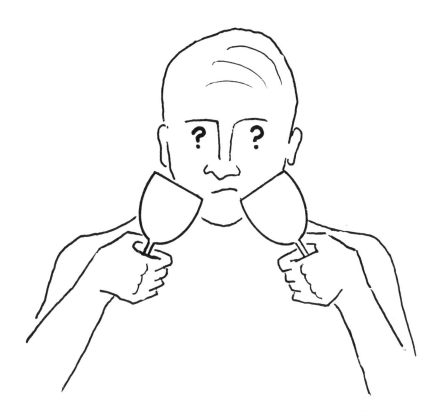

In talking with the these tasters later, I often found that,
in spite of the evidence of their own taste buds,
many of them felt only that they had been "fooled"—
this was repeatedly the word—by the California wines.
The intimation was that they couldn't be "fooled" twice.
Only try to get them to put themselves to the test again!

I long ago got over being angry at their self-hypnosis.
"It's their loss," I said to myself, and took comfort
in the words of 17th Century Mathew Henry, who wrote,
"None so blind as those that will not see."

Did they have blind tastings back in those days, too?

MAY, 1966

CHAMPAGNE

The young lady next to me said, "Pardon me, my feet hurt.
I'm going to see if I can find a place to sit down."
Champagne glass in hand, she left me standing there,
in the middle of a group of other happy Champagne sippers,
suddenly conscious that *my* feet hurt, too.
Just as suddenly, I became aware of a brand new concept
about Champagne—it was a stand-up drink.

Since that discovery, I've been casting back in my mind,
trying to envision the varied circumstances and settings
in which I have consumed Champagne in the past quarter century,
attempting to recall if, on any of these occasions,
Champagne was offered me as a "sit-down" drink.

Not a single such circumstance came to mind.

Anniversary parties? The dinner at the table, of course.
But the preliminary Champagne drinking? Stand up affairs.
Formal openings of new offices or buildings? Stand up.
Wedding receptions? Stand up. Ship launchings? Stand up.
Champagne parties for authors? Stand up. Etc., etc., etc.

How did this come about? What has persuaded party givers
that Champagne can only be enjoyed while on one's feet?

I think the industry itself is responsible for this concept.
Through the vintners' efforts, as a group and individually,
Champagne has come to the point where it is regarded
as an "occasion" drink, a celebratory drink, a commemorative
drink. It's almost never thought of as a pleasant beverage
which can do so much to complement a dinner.

True, I have on occasion observed Champagne being served
to a small dinner group at a swank restaurant. But the fact
that such a circumstance always calls my attention—and the
attention of other diners—to that particular table,
indicates how rare this is.

Today, I checked through a number of Champagne advertisements
to see if any showed people enjoying the wine at the table.
I couldn't find even one. Mostly, the ads just showed bottles.
But where they offered illustrations of people imbibing,
these were shown—to no surprise on my part—standing up.

In Champagne, then, the industry has a low-alcohol beverage
that in usage fits mainly into the cocktail classification.
Since cocktail parties are generally crowded, stand-up affairs,
it's no wonder that I do my Champagne drinking on my feet.

Let my feet complain. I *like* Champagne parties.

JUNE, 1966

OVERPOPULATION

Pinch a social scientist and you've pinched a man
who is firmly committed to the worry that, by the year 2000,
the world will be overpopulated. I'm not going to argue
with this concept, though I will say in my own defense
that my wife and I feel absolutely no guilt in this matter,
having contributed only two offspring to the world,
as sort of replacements for us, once we're gone.

My own worries have little to do with the year 2000.
My immediate concern is with the sad way in which the world
is *already* "overpopulated"—with grape vines.

In 1965, these vines produced some 7 billion gallons of wine
—equal to 2 plus gallons for every person on this planet,
the actual figure depending on how procreative the people
of the world have been since the last population estimate,
a matter of some years ago.

As all readers should know, the United States (mainly through
the overwhelming generosity of the vines growing in California)
last year contributed its bit to the world's wine surplus,
and is almost certain to repeat during the current vintage.
But this nation's production of a mere 250 million gallons

is as nothing compared to France's 1.8 billion gallons,
or even to second place Italy's 1.7 billion gallons.

Nevertheless, every little bit hurts, and no matter
to which wine production country you turn your worried eyes,
there (with the possible exception of Germany) you'll find
the vines producing more wine than the people are drinking.

So everybody says, "Export!" and everybody looks around
to see if they can't unload their surplus on the people
of some other country, be it wine producing or non-producing.
If it's a producing country with its own surplus, what matter?
Give it a bigger surplus! As for non-producing countries,
many of them have been so universally made the targets
for wine dumping that they too are at the surplus point.

I lay the blame for this world surplus on an odd concept—
that wherever grapes grow, the vintners appear to feel
that every last ton, every last berry *must* be made into wine.

I will count the day the vintners throw out this nonsensical
concept as the day the industry can lay claim to maturity.
For on that day, the world will begin to depopulate itself
of vines—and perhaps by the magical year of 2000,
the world's wine supply and people supply will be in balance.

JULY, 1966

113

LUXURY

I suppose when you get right down to the basics,
everything beyond that which is required for bare subsistence
can be labelled as a luxury. And when you consider
how little of that which you have become accustomed to
is actually required to keep you alive and even well,
you begin to realize how luxurious your life is.

What this editorial concerns itself with, however,
is a luxury most of you don't even realize you possess
— the luxury of irresponsibility.

The phrase is not mine — I wish it were.
It was voiced by a legislator who was discussing the ease
with which so many of his constituents arrive at answers
to problems which he, as a solon, must sweat over.
The point he was making was that, if you are not going
to be held responsible for the results of your judgment,
it's no trick at all to find an answer to almost anything.

Every year — every month, it sometimes seems — some group,
some committee, or some board within the wine industry
is faced with the need for making an important decision
which will have a greater or lesser effect on all the vintners.
Because such decisions are hardly ever to universal liking,
those who have the responsibility of voting *Aye* or *Nay*
are later often made the target of a variety of charges —
"What a stupid move!" . . . "Didn't they stop to think?" . . .
"It would have been much better if . . ." Etc., etc.

Maybe, sitting back in your office chair after the fact,
you yourself have made such charges; made them vehemently,
made them in the moral certainty that you were right.
If you've been human enough to do this, you were —
believe me — enjoying the luxury of industry irresponsibility,
since *your* "solution" would never have to face reality.

Mind you, I'm not saying that you were wrong to criticize;
every human action is subject to critical evaluation.
I'm merely saying that it's mighty easy to proclaim,
"I have the answer!" when the answer isn't going to be tested.

The point I'm trying to get over is simply this:
Either take on your share of the responsibility of making
industry decisions or — if you don't care to or dare to —
accept the decisions of those left to make them for you,
while you continue to go about your private business
in the lap of luxury.

AUGUST, 1966

ECONOMIST

In a very practical sense, my wife is a home economist.
In shopping, she looks first for items which will give her
more than 100 cents worth for her dollar. Lacking these,
she's satisfied to get an even break for her money.
But offer her less for her dollar than she thinks the dollar
should buy, and she becomes articulately indignant.
Not only with the retailer but with me too, as if I
were in part responsible for this price inflation.

Lately, I've been having a hard time of it.

It seems the price of everything a housewife needs
(especially food) is rising so steadily that it's tough today
to get a fair shake in what my wife calls this man's world.
Being a man, I'm asked how do I account for this?

In my efforts to placate my wife (for a house without a spouse
is not a home), I've tried all sorts of reasonable answers—
the Viet Nam war, inflation, tight money, taxes, etc.
The last time, though, I threw away excuses, saying brightly,
"Well, at least wine hasn't gone up in price."

The fact is, of course, that it has. But on the average,
the increase has been so moderate compared to what has
happened to other necessities, that wine essentially remains
what it has been for a long time—a real bargain.
I know this because, having made such a dramatic point of it
with my wife, I decided to look up the facts.

First, I checked the California price book for August 1950.
There, I found such representative popular brands
as Gallo, Guild, and Italian Swiss Colony consumer-priced
at 72 cents a fifth for dessert wine, 59 cents for table wine.
Next, I sought out last month's prices for these brands.
I found them posted at 82 cents and 72 cents.

So, all right. Wine prices *are* higher. I admit it.
But compared to what has happened to practically every other
food item? Table wine up 13 cents a bottle in sixteen years.
Dessert wine up 10 cents. This is inflation?

The only inflation that has taken place is in wine quality.
Today's wines are far, far better than their 1950 counterparts.
It's this quality that the added cents are really paying for.

Now aware of this, I feel I can, with clear conscience,
speak right up and claim that—as regards wine, anyway—
today's shopper is getting more than ever before for his money.

Wait until I tell my home economist *that*:

SEPTEMBER, 1966

117

RETAILING

I resent what's going on in retailing today.

Taking my town as an example, here's what I see.
Gasoline selling on the appeal that "You may win up to $5000."
Supermarkets offering customers a chance at a $1000 jackpot.
Cereal firms providing coupons in their packages
worth a cash return to you as purchaser, or entitling you
to buy dishware, knives, toys, etc. at reduced prices.
Practically everybody, except maybe the undertaker,
offering trading stamps in exchange for your patronage.
This is retail *merchandising?*

I doubt if you can conceive anything farther removed
from the "better mousetrap" merchandising philosophy
of days gone by. It seems that it is no longer good enough
to say to the prospective buyer—as the vintners have been
saying for so long—"Here's something that will give you
more pleasure, something that will taste better, something
that will make your home entertaining easier."
No sir. The big and almost universal retailing pitch
today is something quite different—cash. A chance to win
some cash or to get some of your expended cash back.

A professor of economics recently pointed out
that successful merchandising in the U. S. does not depend,
and maybe never did, on the promotion of the inherent qualities
of a product. Rather it depends on the promotion of an *image*
(youthfulness, success, virility, etc.) that can be attributed
by at least a part of the public to the use of that product.
At the moment, as a lodestone to buying, these images
seem to have lost out to that of M-O-N-E-Y.

People who, if you can recall the ads of another and simpler
merchandising period, would "walk a mile for a Camel,"
today will drive several miles in order to shop where they
have a chance—the slim *chance*, mind you—of pulling
in some kind of monetary reward.

It may be that this doesn't bother you at all,
but as I noted at the start of this piece, I resent it.
I resent having a gasoline mogul or a supermarket chief
or the merchandising head of a local department store
figure that I am donkey enough to trade with him
just because he dangles a chance-to-win-money carrot
in front of my nose.

I resent his knowing me that well.

NOVEMBER, 1966

NEW YEAR

I guess, after all, that I'm a pessimist.

For proof, you only need know that, as you and I come to the end of another calendar year, I find it hard to believe that what's ahead of us is going to be better than what's behind us — and what's behind us ain't much.

I believe this is in spite of the many voices raised to say we're right on the verge of a bright new world.

These voices cry that we'll soon be able to fly anywhere twice as fast as today (and, thank goodness, come back equally as fast); that electronic machines will before long relieve us of much of the work at which we earn a living (and which many of us enjoy doing); that we'll be able soon to visit a planet or two; that our telephones will shortly show us the faces of those we're talking to; etc., etc.

All these gains — and they are gains, I guess — are sure
to come before too long. I'll grant that.

Why, then, am I so reluctant to accept the future
as offering us a better life than does the present?

The reason is a simple one. As I look at the troubles
which have enveloped the world back through the centuries,
it seems to me that not one stemmed from a lack of advance
in such areas as transportation, mechanization, etc.
Rather, the world's troubles appear to have sprung
almost solely from a lack of advance in quite another area
— in the ability of people to get along with people.

Even in these "advanced" times, in this last month of 1966,
do I see men taking any real steps towards mutual understanding?
Nothing of the sort. I see war that isn't called war; I see
nation confronting nation, I see man-to-man strife within
our own borders. Does this promise well for the future?

If I were a bright young man looking at the future
and hoping to make a better world, what I would concentrate
on improving is not the jet plane, not the electronic monster,
not the devices by which engineers and mathematicians and
chemists seek to create a practical and economic Utopia.
No. What I would concentrate on trying to improve
is the relationship of man to man.

Once this was accomplished — once even the slightest gain
in this direction was made — I'd be delighted to raise
my glass to yours in anticipation of a Happy New Year to come.

But for the year 1967?

DECEMBER, 1966

BARGAIN

In wine, I'm not a bargain hunter.

At least, not in the sense of being someone trying to find
an absolute top quality European wine at a very low price
under one of those waiting-to-be-discovered brands.
That's a pursuit I gave up many years ago.

There are plenty of people, however, who seem to feel
that searching for a great European wine at a giveaway price
is a worthwhile expenditure of time, energy, and money.

These are people, I've learned, who tend to believe
the enthusiastic advertising adjectives so often used to
describe such low priced wines. They are people seeking a
chance to tell their guests smugly, "Look at the buy I got!"
They are people smitten by rich-looking foreign labels
which must surely, they fondly hope, represent quality wines.
They are people, in a word, who are optimists, pure and
oh! so simple.

Consider the assumptions such wine bargain hunters make,
without even being aware that they are assuming anything.
First, they assume that the vintner underpriced his wine
because he didn't know how good the wine actually was.
(If a winemaker doesn't know *that*, how can you trust him
to know anything at all about wine?)

Next, they assume that the European shipper who bought the wine
from the producer also didn't recognize its greatness;
or having recognized it, underpriced it because his brand
was unknown in the U.S. (And would you believe *that?*)

And they assumed, too, that the importer, who presumably knows his
business, failed completely to recognize the worth of the wine,
since if he had, he would surely have boosted the price
well beyond any bargain classification. (Like most of us,
the importer wants to *buy* bargains, not sell them.)

To call the above presumptions far fetched, is not fetching
far enough, on the basis of my own wine buying experience.
Low priced foreign wines, I've found, are offered as such
because that's all they're worth in the opinions of the
trained professionals who grow them and handle them.
Often, that's more than they're worth.

So if there's a lesson to be learned here, class,
it is that, among the unknown foreign brands (and there are
thousands), the good wines bring the good prices they deserve,
and the bargain hunters get exactly what *they* deserve.

JANUARY,1967

123

EQUALITY

Under the law, we are all born equal. But once born,
equality appears to go out the window.

Don't worry; this is not a civil rights outburst.
Except to point out that the people of the various U.S. states
have a range of personal freedoms that are provably unequal
(for better or for worse) to those enjoyed by the people
of others of the fifty states.

As proof, I need only cite differences in the amount
of hard-earned money the varying state income taxes permit
the resident to keep, differences in the speeds at which
he is allowed to travel, differences in age of consent, etc., etc.

In our field, note the variances in hours when a person
may buy a bottle or a drink, or for that matter *where*
he may buy, and even at what *age* he may buy. Equality?

Responsible for these varying patterns of personal liberties are the elected and appointed lawmakers of the various states. Today, these same lawmakers, apparently not at all disturbed by the fact that equality in many important facets of life does not exist for their people, have embarked on efforts to bring their residents equality with all other U.S. residents in a rather odd — and comparatively unimportant — area: in what they pay for alcoholic beverages.

If the purpose of these efforts is, as I presume it to be, to protect the interest of the man in the street by making him in this regard the equal of all, it is effort doomed to failure.

Doomed to failure not because the states may not be able to force the industry to comply, but because the lawmakers of the individual states have themselves made such equality in consumer pricing of alcoholic beverages *impossible,* even if suppliers were to set fixed national fob prices.

They've done this by making taxing, licensing, and labor conditions in the various states so different from each other, and by establishing (in the control states) such varied markup patterns that, no matter what the lawmakers now do, national equality in consumer pricing of alcoholic beverages will remain nothing but a dream.

And as for the alcoholic beverage industry, its claimed right to do business on terms equal to those offered other industries will also remain a dream.

Or is nightmare a better word?

FEBRUARY, 1967

125

EXPERT

When my wrist watch goes haywire, as it occasionally does,
I take it to a man whose business card describes him
as an expert watchmaker. When my wife has a dress altered,
the woman who does the work has a little sign in the window
in which she calls herself an expert dressmaker.
In a vast number of fields, people who feel they are competent
don't hesitate to use the term "expert" to describe themselves.

No one describes himself as an expert wine judge.

Does this mean there are no judges worthy of the term?
Not at all. Like you, I personally know a number of them.
But ask any one of them if he considers himself an "expert,"
and you're more likely than not to get a stony look,
or some comment saying more or less politely, "Don't be stupid."

You mustn't take this to mean that a good judge of wine
will get mad if *you* call him or describe him as an expert.
He's as human as you are. He just won't label himself such.

I rate this as being pretty unfortunate. If there is no one,
even among those of obvious competence in judging wines,
who will call himself an expert, what can lesser wine judges
(and all imbibers are, willy-nilly, judges) call themselves?

Me, for instance.

I have certain inadequacies of smell and taste memory
which stand in the way of my being a truly good wine judge.
But after 25 years of close contact with wines and vintners,
I have *some* capacity, even if limited, for judging wines.
My problem—and yours?—is how to classify myself.

People often assume that I'm an expert wine judge.
It embarrasses me. I don't know what to say. I can't say
I know nothing about wine because I do know *something*.
Nor, and this is what hurts, can I describe my judging abilities
as "fair" or "passably good" or "reasonably competent"—terms
which might apply—because the experts themselves use these
and similar terms to modestly describe their own capacities.

EXPERT

This leaves practically no adjectives for lesser judges.
So to save me, and others like me, from real embarrassment,
I plead with each of you who is a top wine judge to admit it,
to come right out when asked and call yourself an expert.

Remember, men, there's always room at the top. Move up there.
It won't hurt you, and it will leave us lesser judges
a bit more adjectival elbow room to describe our own abilities.

Lebensraum!

MARCH, 1967

MEDICINE

I've had my share of illness. On such unfortunate occasions,
I've taken pills, or swallowed powders, or drunk spoonfuls
of medicated liquids (the prescriptions for which must, I swear,
have specified in Latin, "Make bitter as possible"). I've also
gargled with Listerine, rubbed Ben Gay on my chest, inhaled
Mentholatum—in short, used as personal medication almost
every nostrum conceived by physician, pharmacist, or wife.
I have never, though, imbibed wine for its medical values.

Why not? Maybe it's because I personally find it difficult
to think of wine as medicine. I *like* wine, and who can like
medicine? Yet its use by physicians is an old, old story.

Even back when bloodletting was the latest thing in medicine,
there were those who thought wine could cure almost anything.
Sure, some claims made for wine in those far-off days
sound fantastic in view of what's common knowledge today.
But the groping doctors of centuries ago knew that, in wine,
they had something that provided a sense of better being,
that offered certain reliefs, and that benefitted their patients
in a number of ways, even if it did not actually cure
all of the ailments for which it was prescribed.

Certainly, no doctor today believes, as did 13th century
Arnald of Villanova, who called himself "Physician, Surgeon,
Botanist, Alchemist and Philosopher" (and could have added
"Author" since he wrote the earliest printed book on wine),
that certain wines could "fortify the brain," "bring back
the memory," "remove defects of vision," "beautify women,"
and do even more wonderful things.

Nevertheless, as modern doctors and medical researchers delve deeper into the use of wine for the sick and the aged, they are finding a constantly widening area of human illnesses in which this beverage, while not the magical cure-all it was rated by the physicians of the 13th century, is an increasingly valuable medical tool.

Knowing this, I hope the next time a doc says "Tsk, tsk!" to me, it will be because I have one of the growing list of illnesses for which knowledgeable medical men today prescribe wine. For, after having taken everything else for curative purposes, wine as medicine now has a wondrous appeal. Prescribed for me ("One or two glasses, to be taken internally twice a day"), I can promise the doctor I'll follow his orders faithfully.

Even, mind you, after I am cured.

APRIL, 1967

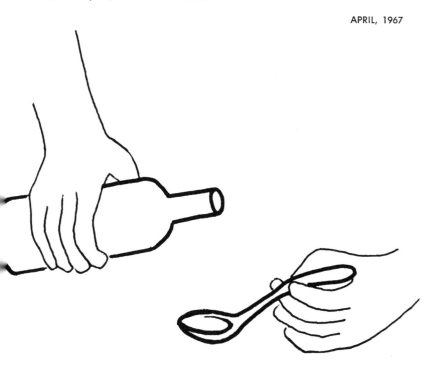

129

VINTAGE YEAR

You've heard it a thousand times:
"Every year is a vintage year in California."
True? False? Willful self delusion?

With the current season off to one of the worst weather starts
in the post-Repeal history of the California wine industry,
maybe now is a good time to check the state's "vintage" boast.

Let's get a couple of witnesses on the stand.
First, the believer: "California's vineyards are blessed,
by and large, with mild winters, good rains during the spring,
warm summers and autumns, and generally clear weather at harvest.
The result is that, year after year, grapes reach the wineries
at full maturity, making wines worthy of vintage designation."

Next, the disbeliever: "Come, now. There's no such thing
as year-by-year sameness in temperature, rain, or sunshine,
even in California. The state has its frosts, its share
of poor summer sunlight, even damaging rains in the Fall.
These are bound to affect the quality of the grapes,
and without quality grapes, vintage wines are impossible.
Some vintage years in California, yes—but *every* year?"

In the light of these pros and cons, let's look at France,
where every year is definitely NOT a vintage year.

The French would be the first to admit that their climate
is often harsh on their grapes. So when, in sharp contrast,
a decent weather year comes along, the French cry "*Voila!*",
put a date on their bottles and invite the world to rejoice.

Good enough. But when a year is rated "vintage" in France,
this doesn't make it a mirror image of previous "vintage" years.
The French themselves rate one such year as better
than another and perhaps not quite the equal to a third.
They know that, even within the range of what they consider
"vintage" years, there are *differences in climatic conditions*
which affect the grapes and, naturally, the wines.

Now back to California. Here, too, there are variations
in climate and consequent differences in grape quality.
But Nature is gentler in California than it is in France.
So if you were to take the measure of grapes delivered
to California wineries, you'd find that, year after year,
they would be well within the quality range that,
in France, would win a "vintage" accolade.

That's all the California vintners are saying.
Is it too much?

MAY, 1967

. . . UH . . .

Champagne is a fighting word to the French producer
of the product of the same name—when that word
is used by producers in countries other than France
to describe the effervescent beverages they make and sell.

Says the French producer: "There's no such thing as California
Champagne, or New York Champagne, or Ohio Champagne.
There is only *one* true Champagne—and only we make it."

According to the French, an American vintner may do everything
the French vintner does in making his effervescent wine,
but since he's not doing it in a particular corner of France,
he doesn't have any right to call it Champagne.

When he does, they charge, he's deceiving the Average American,
since the latter believes—*naturellement!*—that any wine
called Champagne is a product of la belle France.

He does? The French must know different Average Americans
than you or I do. To prove this, simply go out on the street,
tap a passerby on the shoulder and ask him what Champagne is.
If he answers you at all (you know those Average Americans),
it will probably be to say, "Well, it's . . . uh . . . a sort of . . .
uh . . . bubbly wine." And that's it.

Then, because the French make such a point of rating geography
important, you might ask your man, who has already told you
what Champagne is, if he knows WHERE Champagne is.

It may be that he'll answer, "France," and you'll know
that you have before you an educated citizen of the world.
More likely, though, he'll say, "Illinois," for which answer
he also earns an "A" in geography. But the heavy betting
is that he'll say he doesn't know—and he may even add,
"Why don't you ask the cop on the corner?"

There, with maybe a permissable iota of exaggeration,
is the Average Man on the average street in the U.S.

Me, I'm not average any more than you are.
I *know* there's a district in France called Champagne
(though the French mispronounce it "Sham-*pahn*-yeh").
And I know as well that there's a Champaign in Illinois.
Yet if someone mentions the word "Champagne" in my hearing,
what it brings to mind has nothing to do with geography.
What the word means to me—and to you and to practically
everybody else in the entire United States, is . . . uh . . .
a sort of . . . uh . . . bubbly wine.

What else *can* it mean?

JUNE, 1967

BEST

If there's one question I hate to have thrown at me,
and lately I've been hearing it with surprising frequency,
it's, "What's the best wine in California?"

I always take it for granted that the people who ask this
are comparatively unsophisticated imbibers of wine.
Neither the connoisseur nor the pseudo connoisseur
would ever pop that question. In my experience, each of these
has his own definite opinion as to what he rates as top wines,
and neither needs to ask me anything to know he's right.

And right he is. For *himself*.

There is no wine — be it from California, from New York,
from France, from Germany, or whatever country or region
— that is the "best" wine for everyone.

It floors me that people can't recognize this simple fact.
So when I'm faced with the nonsensical question, quoted above,
I usually reply, "There's no such thing," which wins me
anything from an "I beg your pardon?" to a plain, "Hunh?"

I then ask, "The best wine for whom? For you? For me?
For a beginner? For someone who has spent his adult lifetime
studying and tasting wines all over the world?"

At this point, I give myself a hundred to one odds I can
guess the follow-up question, and so far I haven't lost.
It's this: "All right. Which wine do *you* like best?"

They think they have me.

But I'm not as easy to pin down as all that.
"As of this moment," I reply, "I don't know. I've had a number
of good wines and even some great wines from . . ." and I reel off
the names of a substantial number of wine brands, including
some of the so-called "standard" brands. "But," I end up,
"which of these wines would please me most right now,
is something I can't honestly tell you."

What I try to get over is the idea that it's senseless
for someone to depend on me or anyone else to provide him
with more than a general guideline to good wine. After that,
it's up to the individual taster to experiment and find out
which of these wines, or which un-named wine, brings
the greatest gustatorial pleasure to his particular palate.

If he takes my advice, he's got a good start towards learning
to make his own decisions about wine instead of going around
asking such silly — and unanswerable — questions.

I wonder: Which *is* the best wine in California?

JULY, 1967

FRIENDLY

I have, on too few occasions to be proud of,
called a waiter over in a restaurant where I was dining
and selected a bottle of wine to be sent to friends
dining at another table, to be delivered with my compliments.
I have had the same courtesy extended to me and my party,
again rarely enough to make the occasion worth mentioning.
My worry for today is: Why doesn't this happen more often?

Were you to see an acquaintance at the restaurant bar
while waiting for a table, neither you nor he would think it
unusual for one of you to offer to buy a round of drinks
for the other and for his party, should he have company.
But once inside the dining room, seated at a table,
the concept of buying some one else a bottle of wine
hardly ever enters anybody's mind. Why?

Surely it can't be the expense. At today's bar prices,
buying cocktails for, say, four persons in a friend's party
costs as much as buying a bottle of wine to serve the same four.
If a man can afford one, he can afford the other.
So money does not appear to be the basic consideration
in the failure to make this social gesture.

It must be that people simply don't *think* of it,
and perhaps the vintners themselves are to blame for this.
I can't recall a single promotional piece or advertisement
by either a winery or the Wine Advisory Board which made a point
of the inherent friendliness of this kind of gesture.

Too bad. This simple courtesy is one of those things
that brings pleasure to both the donor and the recipient.

Ever notice what happens when a gift bottle arrives?
There is a little buzz of excitement, followed by a craning
of necks by those at the table in the direction of the donor,
with smiling face met by smiling face and a wave of the hand.

The donor cannot help but be aware of the excitement
his gesture has brought, any more than he is unaware that he
has become the subject of conversation at the other table,
and if this pleases him, it's a vanity most of us possess.

As for the recipient of the bottle, upon its arrival
with the quietly delivered message from the waiter,
he becomes a Somebody in the eyes of his dining companions,
with even his wife feeling proud of him.

All this widespread pleasure for the price of a bottle of wine.
Shame on you (and me) for not doing this more often.

AUGUST, 1967

AH, YOUTH

Youth appears about ready to take over the nation,
and whether you look on this prospect with satisfaction,
worry, or horror, I believe you'll have to admit
that this is a fair measure of the current U.S. picture.
The question is: Is the nation ready?

Maybe as a whole, it isn't. But the wine industry is.
Or if it isn't completely ready, it at least has not been
caught napping in preparing for this prospective takeover.

Think back to the talks on wine merchandising and marketing
delivered over the past ten years by various wine industry
sales chiefs. Practically all of the speakers, you'll recall,
themed in on a single target — the young adult.

Recall, too, the illustrated wine ads of the past decade.
Most, you'll remember, showed young adults enoying wine
in social atmospheres considered appealing to them.

Check back mentally, also, to the numerous articles on wine
which have appeared in national magazines in recent years.
Again and again, as I'm sure you'll remember, they focused
on persuading the young adult that he can find pleasure in wine.

Wine, said the speechmakers and the ad men and the writers,
is a socially acceptable and a sophisticated drink.
Wine, they said, is a fun drink, a reasonably priced drink,
a temperate drink. Wine, they insisted time and again,
is a *wonderful* drink for young adults.

Were these years of youth-directed efforts wasted?
Not at all. Regardless of how you may rant and rave
at some of the actions, some of the philosophies,
some of the relationships of the young adults of today,
you can't deny that they're a lot more interested in wine
than were their counterparts of twenty, or even ten years ago.

While a live interest in wine on the part of young adults
may not loom large in the universal scale of things,
it's nevertheless an important consideration for those
whose economic future is tied to wine consumption.
For mind you; a man in his early or mid-twenties who likes wine
is, as the actuarial tables will prove, a fine prospect
to be buying wine for some four or five decades into the future.

Four or five decades! When I think of it, I turn a bit green
with jealousy and say to myself, "Ah, youth." And this is not
only because of the wine.

You know what I mean?

SEPTEMBER, 1967

MUSIC

Maybe you've noticed how much more, and how much more often, people are talking about wine these days. I don't mean just vintners, a few of whom have been known not to mention wine more than once every other sentence; I mean the man in the street, or the club, or the living room, or even the kitchen.

While this man and his friends still don't talk about wine as frequently as they do about fishing or football or femmes, their occasional mentions of the beverage raises no eyebrows, as it might have a few years back. I rate this as a tribute to the conversational appeal that wine now possesses.

When people talk about wine, what is it they say?
They sometimes say the damndest things. Like "The best wines
of California are better than the best wines of Europe."
Or "The best wines of California don't hold a candle
to Europe's best." (These are declarations, you'll note,
that are non-dogmatic, non-controversial, nonsensical.)
When I hear either of these statements made, I edge away.
I want no part of a futile argument.

Or they may say, "I don't know anything about wine, but . . ."
and then go ahead and prove, in some hundreds of words,
that they really *don't* know anything about wine.

I'm not saying this to make fun of the wine consumer;
I'm only trying to indicate the positiveness with which people
generally approach wine as a subject for group conversation,
for even the man who apologizes beforehand for his lack
of wine knowledge doesn't really *mean* that he knows nothing,
but says it as a preliminary to offering a positive opinion.

I don't edge away from such an individual. Instead, as I did
recently at a gathering, I point out that there are few experts
in wine—and for very valid reasons. What with some 5000 brands
available in the U.S., with each brand representing some
half dozen wine types, with each bottle maturing at its own rate
—with all these and other variants, I say, nobody can know
all there is to know about wine. Then, as a clincher, I add
as a sort of confession, "All of us are really ignoramuses
about wine; some of us are merely less ignorant than others."

The reaction is instantaneous and almost always the same.
Every one in the group suddenly seems to find that he has
something he wants to say about wine. I stand back and listen
to the talk flow about me: "Wine. . .wine. . .wine. . ."

It's music to my ears.

NOVEMBER, 1967

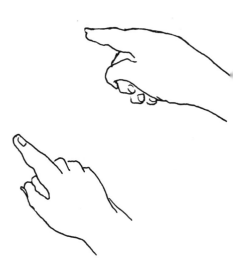

ALCOHOLISM

Alcoholism in this country is a problem. Moreover, it's
one of those problems that won't go away if you just don't talk
about it. So I'll talk about it. Then maybe *I'll* go away.

An alcoholic is more (or less) than just a heavy imbiber;
he is a man who constantly craves alcohol as a thirsty man
craves water. But while the thirst for water is quickly sated,
there's no time when an alcoholic cries, "Enough!"

This literal inability to stop is recognized as an illness.
Whether it is a physical illness, as some doctors claim,
or a psychological one is not for me to say. What I want
to talk about is wine's relation to this illness.

In many minds, wine is intimately associated with alcoholism.
To a great extent this is because, in the nation's skid rows,
the injudicious wine imbiber is highly visible, making some
observers equate wine drinking with alcoholism.

This is nonsense, since it assumes that a man who drinks wine
is automatically an alcoholic. (I know the most dedicated
wine drinkers in the nation in the vintners and winemakers
with whom I have been associated over the past 25 years,
and I have yet to meet the first alcoholic among them.)

I grant that, among the down and outers, there is a percentage
who drink 20% wines solely for their alcoholic content.
I also grant some of these may be true alcoholics.
But alcoholics are to be found in all stratas of civilization,
and most of these rarely if ever touch wine—though they might
be the better off for it if they did.

Actually, today, among the poor, the rich, and the in-betweens,
you find an ever-increasing, even if not overwhelming, number
who *sip* rather than "drink" port, sherry, and other 20% wines.

When I compare these imbibers with the far greater number
who prefer the straight shot, or the whiskey over ice,
or the no-vermouth martini, I can't help but conclude
that such use of 20% wine is more a sign of *temperate* drinking
than it is of intemperance or alcoholism.

As for the skid row drinker, a report issued recently
by the Cooperative Commission on the Study of Alcoholism
following six years of research under a Federal grant, declares
unequivocally: "Skid row problem drinkers (i.e.: wine drinkers)
constitute only a small fraction of all problem drinkers."

What the wine industry has, then, is not the problem drinker,
but the problem *accuser*.

DECEMBER, 1967

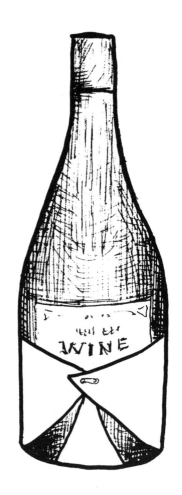

DRY

"Dry" is a perfectly good word.

My first contact with this word came, I suppose,
when I was a babe in arms. My mother: "He's dry."
Since then, I've come across this three letter word
thousands of times, and whenever the word was used precisely,
its meaning was as clear as on the occasion quoted above.
I repeat: When it was used precisely.

For me personally, this word has long had one major
and clearly defined meaning—that the wine it was used
to describe was without sweetness. Check the dictionary;
in reference to wine that is *exactly* what "dry" means.
Some people don't read the dictionary.

Witness. Recently, a friend set out five bottles before me.
They were five brands of a generic wine type. On each label,
the wine within the bottle was described as being "dry."
My friend pointed this out, then poured samples for me.
"Tell me," he said, "which is dry."

Anticipating what was coming, I tasted the five wines.
While I'd be the first to admit I'm not a good wine judge,
I'm not so bad that I can't tell when a wine isn't dry,
no matter what the man who wrote the copy for the label says.

Of the five wines that had been set before me,
I found only one with any real claim to being dry,
if that word is presumed to mean absence of sweetness.

"How," my friend asked when I told him of my evaluation,
"can I have any faith in wine labels if the vintners
play fast and loose with such an important term?"

I had no answer.

Today, the word "dry," in its meaning of without sweetness,
is being used indiscriminately in the wine industry.
Sure, there are some vintners who won't label a wine dry
unless it is really without sweetness. But there are more
who seem to use that term for everything short of Port.
"The public wants it dry only on the label," is their claim.

For their public, they may well be right.
From my point of view, though, this is a sad situation.
A word, be it "dry" or any other word in the language,
should have a definite meaning in the context of its use.
If a word can mean anything and everything, it means nothing.
This is what is happening—has *happened*—to "dry."

Shed a tear for a good word gone wrong.

JANUARY, 1968

BOYCOTT

At this party, I was obviously in over my head.
The conversation flowing around me dealt with international
affairs and I was wise enough to look and listen but not speak.
Then someone turned to me and said, "What's this about
the American vintners advocating a boycott of French wines
in the U.S.?" and suddenly I was not in over my head at all.
I was in fact *it*, with everyone's attention focused on me.

"Not a word of truth in it," I said. With confidence.
Then I began to worry.

The next day I checked to see whether my quick answer
represented actuality or reflected a little dream world of my own.
My checkpoint was a public relations official of Wine Institute.
Certainly, I thought, if any such hanky panky is going on,
these are the people who would be involved in it.

"Last night," I told my public relations contact man,
"Some people at a party suggested that the American vintners
are instigating a national boycott of French wines
so as to get even with De Gaulle. What about it?"

"Not a damn thing to it," was the reply.
So the industry was given a clean sheet, a gold star,
and I was relieved to have my reflex answer backed up.

This doesn't mean, though, that *nobody* is boycotting French wines.
I read of a couple of Congressmen who urged such a step,
and I've seen newspaper stories about restaurateurs in the east,
the west, and the big open spaces in between, who've locked
up their French wines for the duration. More to the point,
I know of a letter to the editor of a Los Angeles newspaper
which not only proposed that everybody quit buying French wines,
but even took the California vintners to task for their failure
to push such a boycott with ads and a full PR program.

Obviously, from what I was asked at the party the other night,
some people believe the industry has been doing just that.
I'm happy to be able to clear the record.

Nevertheless, there may be some readers of this magazine
who of their own accord are suggesting to their acquaintances
that this might be a good time to hold off on the French wines
in order to discover or re-discover the wonderful qualities
the wines of their own country possess. To all of these,
in case there actually are such, I give my assurance
that I don't call *that* a boycott.

That's just good sense.

MARCH, 1968

147

IMBIBING

I don't know what happens to you when you imbibe alcohol.
Likely, you yourself don't know, since it rarely occurs to anyone
to wonder about this part of his life. It occurred to me.

Since it did, I naturally spent some time thinking about it,
and here's what I believe happens to me when I partake.

As a starter, let me note that, with even a modicum of drinking,
I feel more relaxed, I seem to get greater pleasure out of food,
and I become much more tolerant of my fellow human beings
(some of whom require substantial amounts of tolerance to bear).
I rate all these as pluses for me.

What's more, with a reasonable amount of C_2H_6O in my system,
I find that some of the troublesome thoughts of the day
become less disturbing. On occasions, I'm even able to find
an answer to what had previously appeared to be an insoluble
personal, social, or business problem. Another plus.

In addition, others tell me that I become quite jovial,
that I get some needed color in my face, and that I even turn
less argumentative. An almost unbelievable plus, that last.

Overall, then, my feeling about what a reasonable amount of
alcohol does to me can be summed up in one word—wonderful.

Granted, not everyone reacts to alcohol the way I do.
Some of my friends—and yours, too, without doubt—turn
moody on imbibing alcohol; others become gaily effervescent.
Some fall silent; others never stop talking. Some become sullen;
some get amorous; some become pugnacious. Some divulge depths
of emotion and/or intellect I never suspected they had.
And some don't seem to change at all. ("Impossible!" say the docs.)

What appears so remarkable in all this, at least to me,
is that these various reactions come as the result of an intake
(and I don't mean excessive intake) of the same product.

Ask a psychologist why, and he'll tell you that alcohol
tends to release some of the inhibitions of civilization.
With these behavioral bars lowered, the "real" individual
is then free to come out from behind the not-quite-true facade
each of us has been taught to present to the everyday world,
and thus freed, each can "be himself."

Granting this to be as true as the psychologists claim,
it's possible that the only time you or I see our acquaintances
as they really are, is when alcohol has helped them
throw off their restraining shackles.

Let this be the rather horrifying thought for today.

APRIL, 1968

GOOD AS . . .

The other day, I happened to come across a newspaper item
which focused on the increasing values to be found in wine.
Not health values or status values. Money values.
Not surprisingly, the item was on the financial page.

The writer, a business columnist, was reporting on an idea
presented him by the manager of a New York wine wholesale firm
with whom he was discussing inflation and the gold standard.
"Forget the gold standard," said the manager. "To beat inflation,
the best way is to get on the wine standard."

A facetious statement, perhaps, but an interesting one.

Now, I personally have never considered the purchase of wine
as a hedge against inflation. Nor have I given any consideration
to wine as an investment, at least not as a monetary investment.
An investment in pleasure—well, that's another matter.
But it is quite possible that this New York importer is right,
that the way to beat the dollar game is to load up on good wines
when they're comparatively young and comparatively cheap,
to hold them, and each year watch them become more valuable.

I'd just about convinced myself to embark on such a project
when it struck me that wines, like stocks, can *decrease* in value
as well as go up. What's more, since I can't judge which wines,
given a few extra years in the bottle, are likely to improve
and which not, my purchase on this basis would be a gamble
instead of an investment. So I'm having second thoughts.

I realize that I can call on others to help me pick my wines,
but my experiences in this direction haven't been too promising.
Generally, when I've asked a package store owner if a certain wine
I was interested in was ready to drink now or should be held,
the answer has been a wishy-washy, "Oh, the wine is perfectly
ready for drinking now. But there's no reason why it shouldn't
continue to improve in the bottle for the next several years."
Is this a Yes or a No? Should I buy or not?

I must admit that I'm as full of cupidity as the next man.
It would please me very much to set aside a $30 case of wine
and to find, after a few years, that it is worth, say, $150.
Certainly it would please me. But it would disturb me, too.
For should this unlikely but not impossible thing happen,
should a $30 case of wine sitting in my little wine cellar
actually increase in value to $150, I can tell you in all honesty
that I would be faced with a destructively emotional problem—
How can I afford to drink such expensive wine?

MAY, 1968

TRADITIONAL

I know a number of vintners whose proud claim it is
that they make wine in the ancient, the traditional manner.
And they do. Depending on what you mean by "traditional."
Let me put it like this. The original "traditional" way of
making wine was to let Nature do it. Alone. Unaided.
Today, Nature still does it, but no longer completely on its own.

Go back to the beginning. Whoever it was that first discovered
the pleasant beverage that resulted when broken grapes were left
to ferment in some kind of container, must also have discovered
that the beverage, if left alone, would turn sour.

There must have come a day, then, in the time of the ancients,
when someone decided he was going to do something about this.
Whether all he did was to cover the container of wine, or move
it out of the sunlight, is unimportant. What *is* important
is that, in doing this simple thing, in giving Nature a helping
hand, he was "modernizing" the then traditional pattern of making
wine, he was bringing a new dimension to the winemaking process
—he was, in short, becoming the world's first enologist.

From that day on, there have been a notable number of persons
—sometimes uneducated workers with practical cellar experience,
sometimes men of pure scientific bent—who found all sorts of ways
to encourage, change, modify, or otherwise aid the natural process
of winemaking in order to reach increasingly selective goals.

In this manner, the careful selection of grapes, the substitution of known yeasts for the unpredictable wild yeasts, the use of increasingly sophisticated equipment, etc., etc., all slowly brought their changes to the industry. In the passage of the centuries, winemaking became a science, and the winemakers became scientists.

Regardless of innovations, though, there were always some vintners who continued to make their wines in ways hallowed by time, because they believed these were the better, the proven ways. Not for them the latest, the newest, the "modern" methods.

The modern, however, does not remain modern. The new becomes old, and the old may even become hallowed. In the wine industry this has been the case in the past and it will remain so in the future. Fifty years from today, your grandchildren and mine will, I am certain, find vintners boasting that their wines are produced in the traditional way—meaning their wines are being made in the same way they were produced way back in the 1960s.

The traditionalist remains; the tradition changes.

JUNE, 1968

153

HOSPITAL

Let me tell you about my operation.
It happened early this month and, as a matter of fact,
this editorial is being written as I sit up in a hospital bed.
As an operation, what I went through (a skin graft) wasn't much,
but there's a wine angle, so I'll tell you about it.

When I went into the hospital my mind wasn't much on wine.
Then the nurse asked me if I wanted wine with my dinner,
and if so, red, white or pink? I chose the red.
The wine came in a small tumbler of perhaps 6 oz., almost full.
It added considerable pleasure to my dinner. But since I like
to drink a bit more wine than that with my meal, I wondered
how to go about getting it for the next day's dinner.

A check of the menu card for the next day solved the problem.
"If larger portions are desired of any particular dish," the card
clearly stated, "write 2 before the dish." Very good. Only wine
was not on the menu. So I wrote down "White wine," and put a
big circled "2" in front of it, wondering if the declared
concession extended to wine.

When my next day's dinner came, I was delighted. They meant it.
The tray held two glasses of wine. Only this time, instead of being
tumblers, they were small stem glasses of perhaps 4 oz. capacity,
each about three-quarters full. As closely as I could figure it,
my double order had resulted in the gain of one ounce of wine.

While drinking the wine, it came to me that there were other
wine contacts involved in my hospital stay. First, my own doctor
is a determined wine buff, and his partner is the current president
of the San Francisco Society of Medical Friends of Wine.

Second, the skin specialist to whom I went is a man I met
at a wine tasting some years back and in whose office we talk
wine as often as we talk skin. And finally, the surgeon to whom
the skin specialist sent me asked me what I did for a living,
and since I'm not ashamed of it, I told him. Whereupon he said,
"Wine magazine? You must help me select some wines for my cellar."
So, in a way, I was surrounded, at least thematically, by wine.

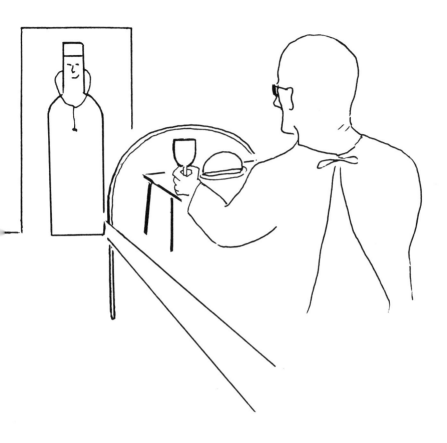

In my short stay at the hospital, I learned something.
The hours in bed go by slowly, and the mind focuses on those
interruptions that mark the passage of the day. Of these,
meals are the most important, and the delight of having something
as pleasant and as sophisticated as wine served with the dinner
made me, and I must admit it, a pretty happy sort of patient.

Well, as happy as I can be in a hospital.

JULY, 1968

COOKBOOK

My interest in cookbooks is somewhat less than overpowering.
Yet, in my editorial capacity, it falls upon me as a duty
from time to time to check into, and to report on,
the contents of a book full of recipes.

My current concern in this regard is the Wine Advisory Board's
newest how-to-do-it: "Gourmet Wine Cooking the Easy Way."
Since my major interest in even looking through a compendium
of cooking formulae is to see what such writings do for wine,
it is obvious that this Wine Advisory Board book can only garner
plaudits from me, and that should suffice as a review.

Now, on to more important things. Like the fact that,
if what I read in the daily papers and the magazines is true,
I am practically un-American in my disinterest in cooking.
Everywhere I turn, photos of men happily broiling steaks for
their friends accost me, and almost every columnist I read dotes
on the way men are taking increased interest in the kitchen.
Are they trying to tell me something?

Personally, my best kitchen role is that of husband-dishwasher,
but since that long-ago day when an automatic device replaced me
(as dishwasher, not as husband) even this limited kitchen chore
has become a thing of the past. Nevertheless, I must shyly admit
that, in my heyday, when I really got going with soap and water,
grease disappeared like magic from the plates, and if some of it
was preserved for posterity on shirt and pants, what matter?

In spite of this attitude on my part, even I am aware
of the way wine has become an increasingly important condiment
(if that's the right word) for those who put together the dozens
of cookbooks that come into the marketplace every year.

There was a time when U.S. cookbooks rarely mentioned wine.
But in this enlightened age, I doubt if a single cookbook author
would dare skip over the value of wine in telling his readers
how to prepare a wide range of dishes from soups to desserts.

This makes me glad, for I like the idea of wine in food,
and if, as I admit, I'm one of those who don't read cookbooks
except under duress, I am at the same time one of those
for whom cookbooks are *really* written. I am an eater.

Why, do you suppose, authors concoct, test, and publish recipes
if it is not to see the fruits of their labor enjoyed?
Enjoyed, mind you, not in the reading, not in the cooking,
but enjoyed in the *eating*. That's where I come in. Happily.

Beats book reviewing any time.

AUGUST, 1968

157

MEMORIES

I've been around a reasonably long time and, like most persons
of my age, my mind goes into reverse every once in a while
and I get to remembering things that were.

I can remember, for example, when $150 was a good monthly salary;
when the 48-hour work week was an acceptable union pattern;
when U.S. wine sales first hit the 100 million gallon mark.

I can remember when a 10-second hundred yard dash won hurrahs;
when the New York Yankees were the scourge of the baseball world;
when Kansas and Oklahoma and Mississippi were legally dry.

I can remember when a "highway" was a two-lane undivided road;
when $1000 was enough to buy a pretty good automobile;
when dessert wine outsold table wine in the United States
by a ratio of better than two and a half to one.

I can remember when girls' dresses drew whistles because they
showed the calf; when padding gave the shoulders of a man's coat
a yard-wide look; when most of California's table wines
were produced in that state's North Coast counties.

I can remember when Liz Taylor was a teen-age movie actress; when Clark Gable made "It Happened One Night," which made him; when a gallon of bulk dessert wine cost up to $1.40.

I can remember when young adult males didn't face an Army draft; when girls wore their hair shoulder length and boys didn't; when bulk dessert wine was reportedly available for 36 cents (and unreportedly for less).

I can remember when it took almost a full day to fly S.F. to N.Y.; when trains were still rated de-luxe means of transportation; when the sale of U.S.-produced sparkling wines set a new record—wow!—of almost ¾ million gallons.

I can remember when George Murphy and Ronald Reagan were Democrats; when Eisenhower was a name few Americans had ever heard; when Claret was a very popular designation for red table wine.

I can remember when "cola" was never used without a "coca" prefix; when a cup of coffee was to be had for a nickel almost anywhere; when U.S. brandy was a beverage going nowhere at all.

I can remember when the Saturday Evening Post cost five cents; when "Time" magazine was born and "Life" came to life; when "Wines & Vines" was competing with rival "Wine Review" for survival as the industry publication.

Yes, I remember these things that were and, in contrasting them to the things that *are,* I must admit that my measure of most of these memories is that I'm glad they're merely that.

SEPTEMBER, 1968

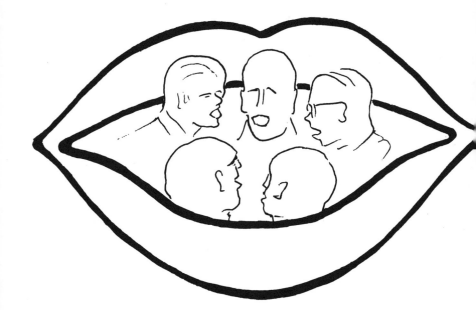

SYMPOSIUM

Symposium? It's "a talking together." Like vintners talking wine,
or lawyers talking law, or golfers talking golf, or even mothers
talking children. So, when doctors hold a symposium, as some are
doing next month in Chicago, they'll talk medicine. Naturally.

Like, for example, wine.

What? Wine as a *medical* subject?
Wine as the central topic at an important medical gathering?
Wine as the total theme before internists, psychiatrists,
gerontologists, gastrologists, and other kinds of -ologists?

Yep, That's what modern medicine has come to.

In fact, today's sophisticated medicine has come so far
—at least as regards wine—that it is nearly to the point
where it was some five hundred years ago, when any physician
who *was* a physician used wine as a magician used a wand.

Certainly, with each passing investigative year, the reach of wine
in treating the sick encompasses a wider and wider field.
Essentially, this is what next month's symposium will focus on,
and since I approve of doctors "talking together" about wine,
I give this symposium a plus mark. From every angle.

I beg your pardon? No, I don't mind telling you why.

First, look at it from the medical viewpoint. The talking doctors
advise the listening doctors how to use wine advantageously,
and this is bound to be good for the patients, no? Yes.

Next check it from the industry viewpoint. No vintner wants
the public to consider wine only as medicine. But it doesn't hurt
to have people know that wine can be good for them, even if they
drink it only for pleasure. Reasonable? Completely!

Now look at it gustatorially. You know, from the taste angle.
Did you ever hear anyone say of a pill he was ordered to take,
"What aroma! What bouquet! What flavor!"? Of course not.
But prescribe wine as his medicine . . . See what I mean?

And now rate it from the monetary, the dollars and cents, angle.
Important? You bet it's important; it's MONEY. Have you paid
for a prescription recently? Now I see you see what I mean.

Next, measure it from the social angle. Here's a medicine
that a sick person can take without embarrassment in company
—and what's more, invite the company to join him. Right?

This time, look at it from the . . . Oh, you're convinced.
You now feel that wine is a proper subject for medical discussion.
Good. I always said you could see things the right (my) way.
And say! Wasn't it fun having our own little symposium?

OCTOBER, 1968

Dear Sir, you Stupe:
I take pen in hand in order
to bring to your attention the
error of y

LETTER

Let someone write something I'm for, and I get to thinking
that maybe I should send him a letter saying I'm with him.
Only, of course, I don't. (You, neither?)
But let that same someone write something I'm against . . .
that's when I *really* think about sending him a letter.
Only, of course, I don't. (You, too?).

Today, however, I went against human nature (yours and mine);
I wrote a columnist a letter. I wrote a man who had, in the past,
said many nice things about wine without hearing a word from me.
Now he has heard from me. It's my hope he wishes he hadn't.

What happened was that this columnist recently made a statement that I felt was damaging to the wine industry, and since I'm a self-appointed brother's keeper (as long as he's a U.S. vintner), I decided to point out to this man the error of his ways.

What got me excited enough to write him were certain opinions he offered about wines that can be labeled "estate bottled," and wines which, under the law, can't use this designation.

Said the columnist: "Less than 10% of all wine is estate bottled." Somebody's guess, but not worth arguing about. THEN he said — listen! — "The remaining 90%, of course, is all *Vin ordinaire.*"

Did you say, "What?!" too?

Hoping to stop future pronouncements of this kind, I wrote him. I said lots of things, but I feel my best argument was to describe two wines and dare him to call them *Vin ordinaires.* The wines:

Wine 1: A top Napa vintner buys young Cabernet Sauvignon wine from another highly regarded vintner of the area, ages it in casks, bottles it and ages it some more, then offers this 100% Cabernet as a 4 year old varietal for $3.75 a bottle. *Vin ordinaire?*

Wine 2: The same vintner buys excellent Pinot Noir grapes from a Napa Valley vineyardist, crushes them, ferments the must into wine, puts it through six years of aging, then offers this 100% Pinot Noir for $4.30 a bottle. *Vin ordinaire?*

Since these imaginary wines can't be labeled "estate bottled," they — and hundreds of other quality wines that really exist — would be classified by this columnist as *Vin ordinaire.*

Silly.

So silly, in fact, that I was foolish to get angry about it. If I hadn't gotten angry, I wouldn't have written that letter. And if I hadn't written that letter, I would have kept my record of not writing to columnists clear and unblemished.

Just like yours is.

NOVEMBER, 1968

BIAS

People who consider me biased in favor of U.S. produced wines
sometimes ask me, "Don't you ever drink any imported wines?"
Since I suspect there are some among you who, given the chance,
would pop this same question, let me answer it once and for all.

The first thing that hits me when someone asks me this question
is that here's a man who just doesn't understand about wine and me.
Here's somebody who assumes that, because I support U.S. wines,
I would rate drinking the wines of another country as a fate
(are you old enough to remember the phrase?) worse than death.

What nonsense. So to keep the record straight, let me advise you
that I certainly buy and drink the wines of other countries.

I'm proud of the American vintner, sure. But I've never said,
nor do I say it now, that only he can make wines of great quality.
There are dedicated vintners in many lands, and some of the wines
they produce deserve the accolades of those who consume them.
I buy their wines and praise them when such praise is warranted.
So do our own producers.

Because of personal preference (and economics), the amount of
foreign wines I buy looms small against my American wine purchases.
But I have selectively drunk, and see no reason why I shouldn't
continue to drink, the wines of Europe, South America, Africa,
and Australia (along with its neighbor New Zealand). What's more,
if you're willing to rate Sake as a wine, then I can honestly say
I've tasted wines from all six of the world's continents.

I want to emphasize this point, since one reason I'm so sure
American wines can hold their own against most of the top wines
produced elsewhere is *because* I've taken the opportunity to taste
and to evaluate the quality wines produced around the globe.

Lacking this comparative base against which to measure our wines,
it would be naive of me to make any claims in their behalf.

In a way, I drink foreign wines out of a sort of business need.
But truthfully, drinking these wines is only occasionally "work";
more often it is a gustatorial pleasure.

As you see, I've opened my heart to those of you who are doubters.
So what've you learned? That I drink both U.S. and foreign wines.
That I like both and praise both. That I can't or won't pick one
over the other as the best in the world. Isn't that about it?

If, in spite of this, you still want to call me biased, go ahead.
Sticks and stones may break my bones but wines will never hurt me.

No matter what country they come from.

JANUARY, 1969

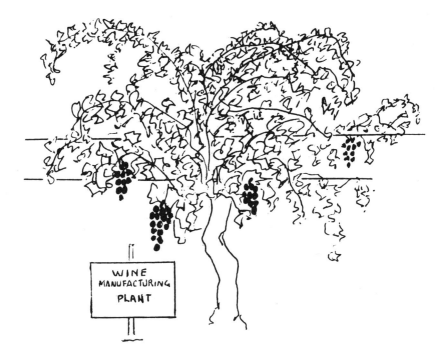

WINE
MANUFACTURING
PLANT

MAD

Show me a man who, from time to time, doesn't get angry
or even explosively "mad," and you show me an angel or a fool.
You can't label me with either name because today I'm mad.

What I'm mad about . . . No, that sounds wrong; it sounds like a
young girl who's "mad about" the Beatles. What I'm mad *at* today
is a word. A single, simple, common word. It's "manufacturer."
Like in manufacturer of wine.

For years, I've seen this me-irritating word connected with wine.
I've read it in newspapers, magazines, even in official documents.
Up to now, I've more or less managed to hold my temper about it.
But when, the other day, I saw this word in print again, it griped me
so much that I felt I'd better get this "thing" off my chest quick
before I became a case for the psychiatrist. So please listen.

Wine, I insist, is not "manufactured." Not in the sense in which I understand the word. Wine may be produced, made, even grown, but not manufactured. How, then, can there be a wine manufacturer? There is only the wine producer, the wine maker, the wine grower. Wine is a natural product. Man doesn't even have to be around in order for Nature to produce this beverage; and if it happens that Nature can't do a very good job of it by herself (she can't) *there* is the real reason for man taking a hand.

He does so, however, not to get in Nature's way but to help her. In no manner does he change the natural process (he couldn't, even if he wanted to) and his ability to help is strictly limited. When Nature fails miserably to do her part, as she did last year in Europe, there's little man can do to make up for this failure. Doesn't this prove that man doesn't have "manufacturing" control? That he simply works along with Nature and hopes for the best?

I realize it's sometimes hard to draw the line between products that are manufactured and those that are not. The yardstick I use is simple: Can and does Nature create the product on its own?

In that sense, to give a trio of simple examples, iron is natural, steel is manufactured; milk is natural, butter is manufactured; wine is natural, whiskey is manufactured. Absolutely clear cut. Is it any wonder, then, that "wine manufacturer" gets me going?

Trouble is, I have only so much "mad" in me, and with the world as it is, I don't want to waste a lot of it on semantics of this kind. So please, everybody, remember that wine may be made, produced, grown—even created—but never, *never* manufactured!

Help me save my mad for other things.

FEBRUARY, 1969

UTOPIA

Each of us has his own separate Utopia, depending on his personal commitment to Life (note the capital "L"). That of a medical man differs from that of a broker, a social worker, a harlot, etc., yet to each the envisioned Utopia is something to be desired.

Seemingly.

Take the American winemaker's Utopia, for example.
This would be a land where Cabernet Sauvignon, Pinot Noir, and other top quality wine grapes would produce 10 tons to the acre, where every ton would easily become 200 gallons of quality wine, where no family would ever sit down to dinner without wine, and where every wine, of whatever brand, would sell at a price that would guarantee a substantial profit to everyone engaged in the production and marketing of the grape and the wine.

Obviously, by this many-faceted yardstick, the U.S. of today is certainly not the wine man's Utopia. Nor does it appear likely that anyone is going to transform the nation into such a Utopia in the near future. In one way, I guess this is a shame. But in another way. . .

Look. Would you really like to live and do business in a land where everything goes right every time without fail, a place that is essentially without challenge? I doubt it.

Human beings being what they are (and while I find fault with some of them some of the time, I wouldn't change them) I believe that each of us would lose something important, something valuable, if everything about us were ideal; if there were no way in which we could improve either our own position or that of others; if there were no "up" carrying with it the threat of "down" to provide the spice of challenge to individual effort.

This type of philosophizing may well reveal a psychological need of my own to constantly prove myself to be what I think I am. If so, I do not necessarily consider it a fault, nor do I believe that I am by any means alone in having such a need.

This, I think, brings validity to the point I am trying to make — that a world of constant challenge (and if history is to be believed, that is what is in store) is not a too-frightening prospect.

Look back on your business, and even on your personal, life. Didn't it consist (among joyful interludes, granted) of a never-ending series of difficulties you simply *had* to overcome? And didn't the finding of a solution to each problem as it arose bring you a deep—*a psychologically necessary*—satisfaction?

There you have your answer to Utopia.

MARCH, 1969

FIRST

Today, I ask you to raise your glass in honor of a man who,
at some time and some place lost in history, was the first
to be invited to dinner and bring a bottle of wine with him.

Granted, we Americans tend to overdo this "first man" bit—
the first man in space, the first man to run a 4 minute mile,
the first man to eat an apple (and didn't he start something?).
But if there were no first man, there would be no second,
and no tenth, and no millionth; and since it's a reasonable guess
that about a million people a year now bring a bottle of wine
with them as a gift when invited to someone's home for dinner,
surely *some* sort of honor is due the man who started it.

I checked into the records feeling sure that somebody, somewhere,
must have previously honored this unknown. Nothing.
I felt that it was up to me.

Before embarking on doing this man homage, though, it came to me
—I'm ashamed to admit it—that he may have brought the wine
with him for a purely selfish reason. Perhaps he was well aware
that his host-to-be had a lousy wine cellar, or no cellar at all,
and guest or not, he wasn't the kind of man who was willing to
sit down to a table without a bottle of good wine in front of him.
He may not—I faced it squarely—have been the complete altruist.

Does this matter, I asked myself. No! I answered myself.
(Lacking company, I often talk things over with myself.)

This having been settled, the question then arose: How honor him?
A medal? Nothing wrong with that, except there was no chest
on which to pin it, no name to engrave on it. How about a statue?
You know, like to the unknown soldier. Not a bad idea at all,
but how sculpt a man whose very dimensions are a complete mystery?
A plaque? Okay, but isn't this the type of thing usually used
to mark a certain spot ("Here, on July 4 . . .") and who knows
in what house, on what street, and even in what city or hamlet
the momentous "first" occurred. You can see the problem I faced.

Yet I was determined to give honor where honor is due.

Then I hit upon the solution. I would suggest to my readers
that whenever they're invited to dinner at a friend's home
they dedicate the bottle they bring (and of course Wines & Vines
readers *always* bring wine) to the first among us to do so.

So I charge you with the execution of this idea. If, in so doing,
in bringing as a gift something that is less caloric than candy,
less dangerous than cigarets, less fragile than flowers, you also feel
virtuous—well, that's one of the penalties for doing right.

APRIL, 1969

MARTINI

It drives me more than a little nuts (no comments, please)
to come across people who ask the bartender for a "Martini"
when what they want, and hope to get, is a shot of straight gin.
Since an unadorned gin drink is now quite acceptable socially,
why can't such persons be honest and simply ask for gin?

I have no intention whatsoever of embarking on an argument
with those who like to imbibe their ethyl alcohol in this fashion.
Drink and let drink, is my motto. What I'm objecting to here
is their habit of hiding their desire for a straight gin drink
behind the skirts of an old friend of mine named "Martini."

In doing this, they have so confused the traditional meaning
of this word, once clearly understood on both sides of the bar,
that those of us who really *mean* Martini when we call for it
(admittedly a declining minority each year) feel that we must
specify to the bartender that we actually want some vermouth used.
Isn't this a hell of a situation?

This complaint is, as you know, a now-hackneyed gripe of mine.
What set me off this time was a recent article on Vermouth
which appeared on the front page of the Wall Street Journal
and which quoted me as saying, re the Martini, that "bartenders
increase the vermouth to stretch the gin after a customer
has had a few and doesn't know the difference."

Far, far be it from me as a reporter to point the finger
at another reporter and claim that I was, by golly, misquoted.
But even if bartenders are in the habit of doing what the reporter
says I said they do, isn't it against all logic to believe
one of them would bare this secret to a patron—a Martini patron?

I am not privy to what bartenders do about the Martini.
All I know is that, when I order one, I keep an eye on the man
to make sure a reasonable amount of vermouth goes into it.
What he does when other people call out "Martini" is strictly
between him and them, my stand being only that it isn't a Martini.
Let them cook up their own name for the drink (Gin-gin?).

A man who can take a "few" non-vermouth Martinis and still be understood when he asks for more wins my reluctant admiration. But I'm not his supporter; he's not my kind of imbiber.

Not for me the 10-to-1, the 15-to-1, even the 20-to-nothing gin and vermouth concoctions. Let those who like them drink them. But you will never get me to admit that such persons—no matter what order they give the bartender—are Martini drinkers.

I am a Martini drinker.

MAY, 1969

AUCTION

The one time I attended an auction (on home furnishings)
it was for the purpose of trying to buy a particular rug
which my wife and I had liked when we saw it at the preview
and for which we felt we were willing to pay a certain amount.
What happened was that I ended up buying the rug, all right —
but at a price well above the previously-agreed-on limit,
and likely above the rug's real worth. I got hell from my wife.

If a number of wives gave their husbands hell following the
wine auction recently held in Chicago (the first such in the U.S.),
I can sympathize with the husbands but agree with the wives.
The wine buyers generally paid too much for their wines.

Too much, that is, if they were buying them solely as *wines*.
If they were purchasing them simply as curios or as rarities,
that's another matter. If they were buying them because they
wanted to be able to show them off in their private cellars,
or to open a bottle now and then in the presence of others
who'd admire them for owning such unusual (if often undrinkable)
beverages, then it's likely the buyers got their money's worth.
Everybody's entitled to get his kicks his own way.

In spite of this concession of mine, you'd have to talk fast
to convince me that most of the winning bidders didn't pay
outlandish sums for their wines. Prices ranged to more than $500
a case, with the final cost (because of import duties, taxes,
shipping charges, etc.) perhaps doubling the winning bids.
At such price levels, it seems to me that the successful bidders
have either over-exaggerated the worth of a glass of wine,
or under-exaggerated the worth of the dollar.

I have a high respect for the dollar and for any individual
who can accumulate enough of them to bid in a case or two of wine
that may eventually cost him $10 a glass at the dinner table.
Cost him that and still leave him unsure, before he tastes it,
that the wine is worth anything at all.

But mingled with this respect is a wonder.
A wonder as to whether any one of the winning Chicago bidders
would have paid the amount he did for the wine he bought
if the wine were available on the shelf of some dealer
and not offered at auction.

My limited personal experience brings me to the conclusion
that logic goes out the window and that reason is destroyed
when an auctioneer voices his first "How much am I bid. . .?"
That is why I stay away from auctions. And that is why I wonder
if some "winners" at Chicago wish they'd stayed away too.

JUNE, 1969

175

TAXES

The Government—that's you and me and the guy next door—
managed to squeeze some $6½ billion in revenue from the nation's
alcoholic beverage industry during 1967, the last year
for which I can find official figures.

Where the government squeezed it from, to put it bluntly,
was from you and me and the guy next door.

From you, if you make and market wines, spirits, or beer,
through fees, licenses, use taxes and a long line of etceteras;
and from me and the guy next door by means of excise taxes
hidden in the prices of the beverages we bought.

Most of this monumental total—second only to income taxes
as the source of dollars to run the various branches of government
—came from the spirits field. Beer, low in alcohol but high
in volume, came in second as an involuntary tax contributor,
with wine third in line at the pay-out window.

Whether first, second, or third, each segment of the industry
paid out a substantial sum in relation to its over-all gross.
Far more than any other single field of endeavor.

What business is this of mine?

Well, sir, I'm glad you asked that question.
It's true that I neither make nor sell alcoholic beverages.
So looking at it one way, it's really none of my business
that the beverage producers have to dish out ladles full of dollars
so that your government and mine can operate. *But . . .*

But while the government collects the taxes from the producers,
I'm one of the millions from whom the dollars *really* come.
The producers, understandably enough, add the tax burden
to the price of their beverages; the wholesaler and retailer
naturally add their mark-up to this amount (they want to stay
in business too), and I as a consumer am the one who pays it.
Since it's my money, I think I have a right to speak out.

To speak out doesn't necessarily mean to complain.
I know that all levels of government are in a monetary mess.
I know that the government has to dig for additional dollars,
and that it can dig only in my pocket and yours. And I also know
that every time I buy a bottle of wine or brandy or whiskey
it may hurt my pocketbook but it helps that of the government.
So I'm not complaining. Not too much.

Indeed, instead of feeling bad, I found myself the other day
regarding wine drinking in a new light—as a patriotic duty.
Do you suppose I'm going mad?

177

100 PERCENT

The subject for today, class, is 100-percent-ism.
I have long been aware that there are, among you consumers,
those who maintain that a varietal wine not made 100 percent
from the grape which gives the wine its name is a phony.

You couldn't be more mistaken.

Don't misunderstand me, class. I'm not saying that vintners
who go the 100 percent route are using poor judgment.
Nor am I saying that you consumers who insist that varietal wines
be 100 percent "pure" are deluding yourselves. Not at all.
I simply believe there's an overemphasis on 100-percent-ism.

Sure, a wine made entirely from a single grape type can be superb. But so can a blended wine. You all know this. Or you should. Certainly the wine producer knows it; and just as certainly he blends or doesn't blend (assuming availability) according to what he believes will put a better product in the bottle. This is important to him because his company lives or dies according to the taste satisfaction his wines give people like you. And it should be important to you because what you're after in your wine bibbing is the same thing — taste satisfaction. Well, the 100 percent road is not the only path to this goal.

In one way, most of you have shown that you know this. Consider. Don't practically all of you laud without reserve the top Bordeaux wines, made of Cabernet Sauvignon grapes but never made 100 percent of these grapes? Of course you do. Why then do so many of you insist that the American counterpart of these wines be made *exclusively* of Cabernet Sauvignon grapes? Aren't you being illogical and perhaps a bit silly?

No raising of hands, please, class. This is *my* lecture. You may demonstrate — peacefully — after you're dismissed.

Besides, I know just what you want to say. That in one case the wine is named for the place, the region, even the chateau, while in the other it's named for the grape. Isn't that it?

It's a good enough point. But what is really important to you? How the wine is produced or labeled, or how it pleases you?

So in this way, class, we come to the lesson for today. Repeat after me: "I will develop a take-it or leave-it attitude towards the 100 percent concept in American varietal wines, and I will use as my sole yardstick in judging the value of a wine the taste satisfaction I get from drinking it."
Very good. Once again, please, and louder.

Excellent! Class is now 100 percent dismissed.

SEPTEMBER, 1969

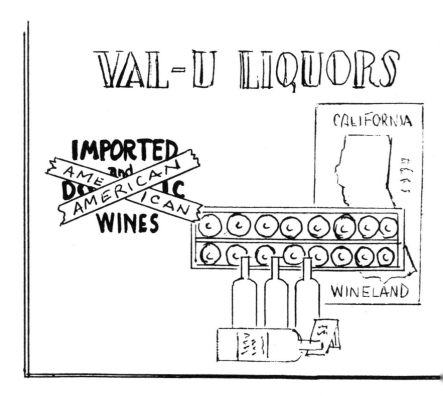

WATCH YOUR LANGUAGE

These are days of language permissiveness,
and what used to be called gutter talk now appears in print,
is spoken from the stage and is mouthed on the movie screen
almost without ending. I want to take my stand on this.

But let me warn you; I'm not going to do what you think.
I am neither going to condemn nor to defend four letter words;
that's for those either more or less sensitive than I am.
Instead, I'm going to give you a *new* word to add to those
you consider "dirty" and I'm going to ask you never to use it
publicly in mixed or unmixed company.
The word: "domestic."

In the substantially different days of the 19th century,
a "domestic" was someone who worked in a rich man's home
doing all the nasty little tasks the elite weren't supposed to do.
The word never had a connotation of quality. It doesn't today,
and that's exactly why I consider it a "dirty" word to use
in describing a product made in the U.S. Like wine.

Evidence that U.S. wines are often described as "domestic"
is to be found almost anywhere you look (except here, of course).
It is my personal habit to refer to a wine produced in the U.S.
as — strangely — a U.S. wine. Or on occasion an American wine;
or more particularly, a California or New York or Ohio wine.
Even, as warranted, a Sonoma, Napa, Lodi or Finger Lakes wine.
Never, *never* as a "domestic" wine.

Unfortunately, many individuals, including some of those in
the trade, don't recognize "domestic" for the dirty word it is.
Result: they often use the term unblushingly: "Here's a nice
domestic wine . . ." Do they think that's a *sales* pitch?

The situation has gotten so bad that, in any number of outlets,
you can even find the word painted on the store window,
right where *children* can see it.

Obviously, I exaggerate. I don't really believe irreparable harm
is done when an American wine is described as being "domestic,"
since I have confidence such a wine can stand on its own.
But I feel that some who use this term (of *course* you don't)
are not fully aware of the psychological negatives involved
and I want to fix a firm "No, no!" in their minds about it.

As for those deliberately using the word for its negative impact,
as some do — well, I don't dare to print what I think of them.
Language permissiveness doesn't extend that far.

But if it ever does . . .!

NOVEMBER, 1969

REPEAL

I've been struggling with this editorial since December 5, 1969.
That morning a local radio announcer reminded me and others
that Repeal had that very day reached its 36th anniversary.
What took this out of the "So what?" class of information for me
was the fact that, in recognition of the occasion, the announcer
presented two separate comments about the Repeal years.

One was a quote from the WCTU president. Her repeated theme
was that Repeal had made us "a nation of 4 million alcoholics."

The second was also a quote, this time from a man described as a liquor industry attorney. What he had to say was that, since Repeal began, the industry he represents has contributed umpteen billion dollars to the economy of the nation.

Both these points have been bothering me since I heard them made. The more I thought about them the more I wondered if either contributed anything important or basic to the core of the question of that day — whether making the sale of alcoholic beverages legal is the best all-round answer to an undeniably real problem.

Let me start by taking up that statement about all those billions of dollars flowing into the coffers of the nation. As a measure of the "rightness" of the legal sale of alcohol, I rate it a nonsensical yardstick. Sure, it's nice the industry provides jobs for many citizens, along with lots of tax money for city, state and federal governments. But that's not what Repeal, when it was voted in, was all about. Rather, its purpose was to give back to the citizenry a liberty stolen from it.

That some take excessive advantage of this liberty is unfortunate. They become the alcoholics the WCTU — and you and I — deplore, the alcoholics the Drys believe they can "save" merely by having the United States placed off bounds to alcoholic beverages.

This, too, is nonsense. An alcoholic is a sick man. For him to get well and remain well requires that he not drink. Everybody knows that. But the decision not to drink must be made by the alcoholic *himself*. Outside decisions — by the doctor, the family, the legislature — will have no lasting effect.

So, as I noted before, I've concluded that neither of the two statements I heard on December 5, 1969 made a real contribution to the basic concept of why Repeal instead of Prohibition. Repeal wasn't instituted to fill the coffers of industry or government, and alcoholism cannot be cured by rule and regulation. Repeal is here because the public wants it. It stays here because the public wants it. Everything else is minor.

JANUARY, 1970

DISCRIMINATION

Discrimination is a pretty nasty word to be mouthing these days.
But that's what this column is all about. Discrimination.

It would be my guess that, what with newsmen, columnists and such
using the word "discrimination" almost daily and almost exclusively
to denote an unfair deprivation imposed on one group by another,
we've lost sight of the fact that this word also possesses
meanings that are good and positive.

If you need concrete examples, let me note that there are real
values in discrimination when applied to art and music.
Or — and this is certainly more down my alley — that there are
many positive things to be said for discrimination in wine.

Before getting down to wine, though, let me talk in wider terms. When, for one reason or another (lack of money, for example) we buy something lesser knowing it is so, that's one thing. But if we buy it thinking it's the *best*, we're cheating ourselves.

Or consider the "all I know is what I like" school of selectivity. In one field or another, most of us are graduates (*cum laude!*) of this school. I may buy clothes, you cigars, someone else wine this way and what's wrong with it? What's wrong is that, if we can't recognize quality as such, we're really choosing blindly.

Now, I don't say that those who buy wine on this guesswork basis are to be scorned. Far from it. There are few vintners indeed who could keep their doors open without sales to the multitudinous followers of this buying pattern. This holds true even of vintners who deliberately aim their wines at those with educated palates.

Inevitably, a certain percentage of such wines are purchased by persons who lack the ability to recognize the nuances of aroma, bouquet and taste which are the proper pride of their producers. In a sense, because the wine isn't fully appreciated, it's wasted. Yet, for a variety of reasons — including economics — a vintner cannot say to the public, "*You* may buy my wine but *you* may not." That would indeed be discrimination. Of an illegal kind.

I'm for legality every time. But I'm also for discrimination in what I consider its best meaning — knowledgeable selectivity.

If you don't possess this knowledgeable selectivity in wine, I urge you to get with it as quickly as you can. Here is where discrimination really pays off. Not only because it helps you get your money's worth. But also because it brings you taste satisfactions such as you haven't experienced before. *Plus* added esthetic pleasures of the kind you shouldn't want to miss.

And — best of all — it hurts nobody.

FEBRUARY, 1970

185

MAN IN THE MANGER

Almost surely, you've never heard of Sim Van Der Ryn.
Neither had I until recently. Yet here I am, writing about him.
Reasons? First, and to me least important, he's a professor
at U.C. Berkeley (and don't tell me you've never heard of *that*).
Second, he's very much interested in wine. And third, he's an
occasional columnist. That last brought him into my ken.

Not long ago, he did a nostalgic piece telling how, ten years ago,
he could make the rounds of California's North Coast wineries
and find himself, glass in hand, in quiet uncrowded tasting rooms
where he could taste at his leisure. Going the same rounds today,
he finds the "glass" often plastic, the rooms crowded and noisy,
and the chance to do what he calls "unhurried tasting" gone.

Van Der Ryn feels that too many people — maybe the wrong people — are filling the wine tasting rooms today, especially on weekends. These persons, he finds, spoil his pleasure in winery touring.

My own recollection of such touring goes back some three decades, to a time when few wineries had special tasting rooms and when visitors were more un- than usual. Back enough years so that, when Van Der Ryn and the thousands of others who "discovered" winery touring the past ten years first showed up, I could have said that their increasing numbers were spoiling MY tasting. I didn't say it. Their being there didn't bother me.

Some people approach wine with near reverence. I don't. I like wine and the better the wine the more I like it. It's as simple as that. I also like people, and the better the people (whatever that means) the more I like them. Even in winery tasting rooms. It, too, is as simple as that. Or I am.

Wine, I believe, has something for all. For the connoisseur and for the neophyte; for the rich and for the not-so-rich; for the few and for the many — and the more the merrier, I say.

For their part, the vintners who cater to and encourage visitors love serious wine imbibers such as Van Der Ryn. No question. But being artists *and* businessmen, vintners also keep a warm spot in their hearts for those who are less knowledgeable, less critical and less staid. But who call on them in numbers. And who buy.

Maybe what bothers Van Der Ryn on his winery rounds is the fact that these others aren't taking wine tasting seriously enough. They're so casual. They talk, joke, laugh. Perhaps even worse in Van Der Ryn's eyes is the fact that they seem to be having a hell of a good time, seem to be finding wine tasting *fun*. Imagine!

MARCH, 1970

187

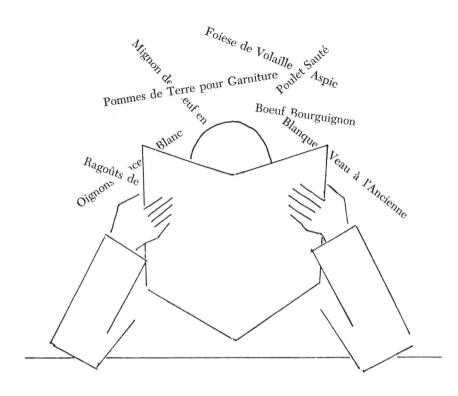

MENU

The other night, dining out with some people in San Francisco, I was confronted with an impressive menu in which the main dishes were all listed in French, a language in which I am close to lost. While, in the past, I've come across such menus innumerable times without its bothering me, this evening I resented it. Aloud.

"Why," I asked, "Can't they call a dish 'stew' instead of *ragout?* Why does chicken have to be *coq* or *poulet?* and beef *boeuf?* What's wrong with using English to describe the dishes they offer? The whole thing is a phoney, a commercial fraud."

"Well, now," said one co-diner, "I see why you call it phoney. But is it as phoney as using French names for American wines?"

Oh-oh, I said to myself, here we go again.

Here come the old pro and con arguments on our use of Burgundy, Rhine wine, Champagne and Sherry. I rate myself a pro at this, but it looked as if this time I had left myself wide open.

Politely, I listened to the usual arguments against industry use of foreign place names for American made wines — it's "deceptive," it's "unfair," etc., etc. I gave him the usual answers.

The strange part of the discourse, at least from my viewpoint, was that my vocal opponent, who respects wine and food equally, didn't have the same objections to the giving of French names to American made dishes. "Not at all the same thing," he said.

From the menu, I picked out a dish, *Boeuf Bourguignon*. The steer that involuntarily provided the beef was almost surely raised in the U.S., I pointed out; the sauce was likely made with condiments grown within the borders of the United States; and the restaurateur, to my knowledge, was born in San Franicsco — of Italian parentage. I then asked my argumentative opponent why he didn't object to this U.S. made dish having a French name.

His answer made sense. Because the dish, he said, had been made from the same kind of ingredients and in the traditional manner in which it was prepared in France's Burgundy district.

I complimented him on his judgment. Then applied it to wine.

Why, then, I asked him — I thought cleverly — isn't a wine made by U.S. vintners in the same manner and under the same guideposts followed by Burgundian vintners entitled to be called Burgundy? His reply carried a that's-enough-of-that tone: "Nonsense."

So this argument ended the way all arguments on this subject end — in a tie, with no minds changed and with each of us certain we held *the* sound position, which the other simply refused to see.

The argument over, we proceeded to order. In French.

JUNE, 1970

BEAUTY

Glamour magazine recently told its readers that drinking wine
was good for their health (pretty old hat now), then casually
threw in the concept that wine also could help them be *beautiful.*
When I learned this, I thought, "Wow, a brand new plus for wine,"
and sat right down at the typewriter to report it.

What was my rush? Listen. I have a habit of taking a good look
at the people I pass on the street daily, and it struck me how
lucky it was for many of them that Glamour had discovered a way
for them to be beautiful via wine. It also struck me how lucky
it was for me, since I'm the one doing the looking.

This, of course, was personal. But I also rated Glamour's find
lucky for the industry because the public spends billions yearly
on beauty aids, in which classification Glamour has placed wine.
True, most beauty aids are for external use—you smear them on,
rub them on, spray them on, paint them on, even paste them on.
Others, though, are meant to be swallowed, which is where wine
fits in, and which is why I felt I had to alert the wine industry
as quickly as possible to this suddenly-discovered market.

In this connection, too, I wanted to point out to the vintners
that the search for beauty is today no longer the sole province
of the female. Every year, men (the backbone of U.S. wine buyers)
are spending more and more money on what, if you want to be honest,
you have to call beauty aids—and with wine being rated as such,
it seemed logical for me to get the good word down on paper fast,
before some other industry writer beat me to it.

But as I got to this point in my writing, a new—and sobering—
thought on the subject of beauty and wine hit me. Hit me hard.
I got up and looked in the bathroom mirror. Here is a face,
I said to myself, that belongs to a man who has consumed wine
with regularity and with pleasure for more than a quarter century.
Where is the beauty that Glamour intimates should be there?

Deflated, I came back to the typewriter and put down these words
about wine as I know it: It is tasteful, colorful and healthful.
It is convivial, pleasurable and relaxing. It builds appetite,
improves digestion and induces sleep. It makes lunch a feast,
dinner a banquet and supper an occasion. It is romantic, glamorous
and an aid to the timidly amorous. It is . . . well, it is so many
things, has so much going for it, that for me to insist it must
be a beauty aid in addition would make me out a fool.

No fool I. But as a steady wine drinker, I can't help thinking
how nice it would have been for me if Glamour had only been right.

JULY, 1970

191

STEMMED GLASS

Some place back in history (and not too far back either) a man
who wouldn't leave well enough alone invented the stemmed glass.
Nobody knows just who this inventor was and nobody knows just why
he put a stem on an already grasp-able container—unless it was
to make holding the glass easier. And even if that was not his
purpose, it's what everybody uses his invention for.

Well, almost everybody.

There are to be seen among wine drinkers a number of persons who scorn the stem as the proper handle for their glass of wine. Instead, they pinch the base of the wine glass from the side, squeezing it between bent forefinger on bottom and thumb on top, in about as awkward a way to hold a glass as can be devised.

Why do they do this? You'll have to ask them. I've asked and never gotten a satisfactory answer. The usual reply is that it keeps the heat of the hand from warming the wine.

I can't buy this. If I recall my high school physics correctly, glass is a very poor conductor of heat and the chances of a finger-hold on a thin stem heating up the wine in the bowl above are so slim as to warrant a thousand to one bet.

Holding a glass by the base, let me inform non-industry readers, is not an industry pattern. For proof, I refer you to the cover of last month's Wines & Vines, depicting the giving of toasts at the annual meeting of the American Society of Enologists. In the photos comprising that cover, I challenge you to find a single raised glass being held by its base.

Holding a glass by its base is, I insist, an affectation (and I say this even though I know that some of my best friends hold their glasses this way). I present as evidence the fact that these same people, when offered a stemmed glass of anything *but* wine, will hold it as most of us do—by its stem.

I understand that holding a glass by its base is widespread among Bordeaux's chateau people, and I can personally vouch that, at Mouton Rothschild one day last month, that chateau's winemaker held his glass of 1969 wine by its base (while I held mine by its stem), so perhaps the base grab is one way for wine buffs to show publicly that they are, in the vernacular, "with it."

Obviously, I'm not. This gives you readers who disagree with me a chance to toss my comments aside disdainfully as those of one who just doesn't understand the need for *form* in wine drinking.

To that, I'll raise my glass. By its stem.

AUGUST, 1970

CONGRATULATIONS

I have, on a number of occasions, sat in on a panel of judges
embarked on evaluating a group of wines. (Don't misunderstand me;
sitting *in* on such a judging panel is by no means the same thing
as *sitting* on a panel; I was there as a reporter.) Anyhow,
I learned at least one thing from these occasional visits—
even among top wine judges there are differences of opinion.

Generally, such differences are minor, but not always.
More than once I've heard a judge say to fellow panel members
who had preceded him in giving their individual measures
of a wine preparatory to reaching an over-all group opinion,
something like, "Someone must have poured me a different wine."
Facetiously said, yes, but his subsequent report proved he had not
been influenced by the uniformly differing evaluations of the wine
given by those who had spoken ahead of him. This impressed me.

Most of us (and by "us" I don't necessarily mean you and me alone,
but the public at large) differ from the above-mentioned judge
in that we *can* be pre-swayed to form a particular opinion
about a particular wine. Swayed in a variety of manners.

Take price, for example. We're all (now, be honest with yourself)
impressed by price. We find it hard to get away from a feeling
that if an item—suit, shoes, candy, wine, etc.—costs more
it must be better. Subconsciously, we've prejudged the item.

Advertising also does its share in making us pre-decide that one
item or brand is better than its rivals. Where an advertisement
fails to do so, it is often only proof that the ad's copywriters
—amateur psychologists and very clever fellows as a rule—
have simply failed to "read" you and me.

There are literally dozens of such pre-persuaders—the host who
tells you "Here's a really great wine," the merchant who displays
a bottle as if it were a jewel, the writer who lists certain wines
as tops, the "quality" label, the term "imported," etc., etc.
It takes a strong will to counter such efforts by the myriads
who are intent on making up your mind for you beforehand.

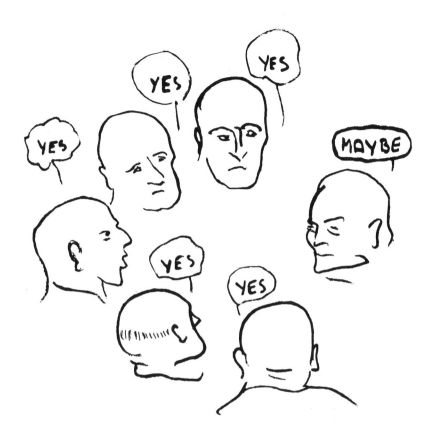

Not one of us is completely free of the effects of such efforts.
But as you know, the enjoyment of wine lies in good part in making
up your own mind, regardless of who said what before you.
When you can get up on your own and with calm confidence offer
the equivalent of "Someone must have poured me a different wine,"
you may be mistaken, sure, but there's no doubt you have proved
you're freer than most from imposed pre-judgements.

Congratulations.

SEPTEMBER, 1970

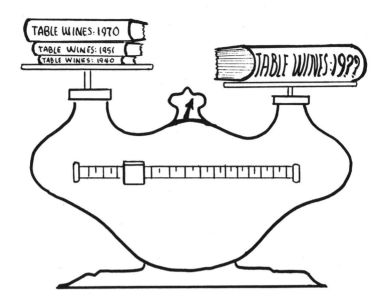

WEEKENDER

Because I came to Wines & Vines as a journalist knowing nothing
about wine production beyond the fact the stuff came from grapes,
I spent the entire first weekend after I got my editorial job
at home curled up with a good book—a real mystery story titled
"Commercial Production of Table Wines," by Amerine and Joslyn.

This little volume, published by U.C. in 1940 for industry use,
gave me at least a beginner's knowledge of winery cellar practices
so that my subsequent writings sounded reasonably authoritative.

That was nearly three decades ago. Yet even today, as I write this,
a copy of "Table Wines" sits on my desk within reach of my hand.
True, this is not the slim treatise published by U.C. back in 1940
and available from the University without any charge whatsoever.
Nor is it the larger "Table Wines," also by Amerine and Joslyn,
published in 1951 by the University and priced at $4.50 retail.
It is, instead, this same duo's considerably bigger "Table Wines,"
published earlier this year to sell at $25.

From free to $4.50 to $25 is one measure of what has gone on
in the American wine industry (and the American economy) in the
three decades separating the first Amerine-Joslyn table wine book
from the third. This, however, is not the important measure.

That is to be found in the fact that in 1940 it took the authors
only 143 pages to put together all the then-available information
on table wine production, while in 1951 they had to use 397 pages
to do an equivalent job, and this year almost a thousand pages.

Since I take this to represent an apparent sevenfold increase
in the knowledge of how to make better and better table wines,
it seems logical for me to conclude that the wine industry has,
in the past thirty years, moved ahead farther and faster
than at any previous like period in its long history.

Who gets a pat on the back for this, I can't tell you.
Except it's no one man or ten men or even two dozen men.
The references cited in the latest "Table Wines" total over 2,000,
reflecting untold hours of research by hundreds of individuals.

You would think that, after maybe a thousand years of research,
just about everything that is to be known about making table wine
would now be on record. Not so. I'll warrant that today
there are researchers all over the world discovering still newer
things about how table wine becomes table wine. Likely result:
the next Amerine-Joslyn "Table Wine" book will top 2,000 pages.

I pity any future new-to-the-industry editor who'll have to spend
his first weekend on the job studying *that*.

OCTOBER, 1970

PROVERB?

Pride goes before a fall. An accepted proverb, no?
No. Not by me. Up to recently, I admit, I neither accepted it
nor rejected it; I was in what you might call a quandary—well,
you might! —and the other day I decided to do something about it.

Here's how I went about it. I listed as many as I could recall
of the vintners who'd closed their doors the past quarter century
and to each of these individuals I applied the concept of pride
to see to what extent I thought this responsible for his fall.
My answer: Not at all. Not in a single case.

Then I took another tack. I listed some of the more successful
of today's vintners and applied the concept of pride to *them*.
Here, among the obviously non-fallen, I found pride rampant.
Ha! I said to myself, whoever it that is pushing the proverb
that pride goes before a fall doesn't know the vintners I know.

These vintners, I found, were proud of their wines. As expected.
But they each had other individual prides—of family, of wealth,
of appearance, integrity, honors won, etc. There were even some
who seemed to be additionally proud merely of being proud—and if
the old saying really *has* anything, this should've meant disaster.
Yet not even these super-proud ones showed any signs of falling.
Ergo, I decided in Latin, something's screwy somewhere.

So I checked further. This time I applied what I recalled of my
high school geometry—the whole of a thing is equal to the sum
of its parts. If today's vintners are individually proud,
I reasoned, then I should find the industry bursting with pride.
Well, that's just the way I did find it. Should I take this
to mean, then, that the industry is headed for a fall? Nonsense.

What is true of vintners may not, I admit, be true of other men.
Yet vintners can't be too different from others, and while I have
stuck solely to them in measuring one aspect of men and pride,
I see no reason why I can't apply my findings universally.

So where am I? Back to whether I should believe or disbelieve
that oft-quoted ancient proverb, "Pride goes before a fall."
Well, I've made my decision. I now *dis*believe it. Or at least
I disbelieve the proverb in its generally accepted meaning.

When I read these words now, I find that they say something
much different to me, something I'm quite willing to accept,
something almost directly opposite the usual meaning given them.
When I read these words now, this is what I see in them—
That when pride *goes*, a fall is inevitable.

Would you accept that as a new proverb? Sort of?

NOVEMBER, 1970

199

IT

Anybody here remember author Elinor Glynn? All of 50 years ago,
she discovered "It." "It" was sex-appeal (a dirty word then),
and Clara Bow, who played the starring role in the Hollywood movie
based on the Elinor Glynn book, became the "It" girl and a symbol
for practically everything considered femininely desirable
in those quite innocent days.

Today, it seems to me, the American wine industry has "It."
From the way aggressive entrepreneurs have been flocking around,
giving the industry the eye, looking into its family background,
courting members of it and even marrying into it, I must conclude
that winemaking, if it doesn't have sex appeal (I think it has)
certainly has profit appeal—a pretty good "It" on its own.

As you may know, this is not the first time non-vintners
have looked at the American wine industry and found it attractive.
A full three decades back, Schenley bought Cresta Blanca and Roma,
National Distillers bought Italian Swiss and other wine properties,
Hiram Walker bought Valliant Winery and the R. Martini Winery,
and Seagram Distillers bought Mt. Tivy and Paul Masson.

However, those marriages of American distilleries and wineries
were not necessarily cases of love at first sight. More properly,
they could be defined as having been liaisons of convenience.
The advent of World War II brought the production of grain spirits
to a practical halt, and the above distilling firms saw, in the
wine industry, an added if limited source of alcoholic beverages.
The result: wedding bells. As with other wartime loves,
some since have faded.

There is, I feel I must point out, a considerable difference
between today's courtship of the industry and that of yesteryear.
Then, it was the desperate need to get out of a hole that made
bridegrooms of the distillers. Today, the major reason for the
courting of the vintners is the indisputable fact that such a
marriage brings with it a substantial dowry—a promising future.
Plus, of course, a booming present. With the latter coming
at a time when other fields are finding the going very rough.

This gives the wine industry a pretty universal "It."
So it's no wonder that the recent benedicts are not exclusively
distilling companies. Or that the still-searching swains
include top firms engaged in a wide range of business enterprises.

I think even Clara Bow, used to adulation as she was,
would not have scorned the concentrated attention so many persons
are now giving the wine industry. It's always nice to be wanted.

Even if it's only for your money.

DECEMBER, 1970

ADVICE

It's no problem at all to find somebody who will tell you what to drink, when to drink, where to drink, how to drink and even whether to drink. Among those who will willingly offer you this kind of advice as a social, moral or legal guide are doctors, bartenders, cops, ministers, the people next door, spouses, members of the WCTU and those engaged in making a living producing the various beverages containing alcohol.

A special addition to this advisorial list is that of writers.
There are increasing numbers of authors of varying capacities
(writing, not imbibing) whose pieces in one publication or another
advise millions on the what, when, where, how and why of imbibing.
Many of these writers concern themselves with wine and its place
in the daily living patterns of those they are addressing,
and for this I thank them. But sometimes . . .

One of the most sincere wine writers I know recently put together
an article on drinking which he titled: "The Secret of Temperance:
Drink Only When You are Happy and Never When You are Unhappy."
This may or may not be sound psychological advice. I hope not.
Because I see in it certain implications that bother me very much.

Understand, my reaction is a very personal one. I enjoy imbibing,
and my usual pattern is to have a cocktail or two before dinner,
plus wine with my meal. If I were to limit this temperate pattern
of drinking to occasions when I am "happy," I can tell you frankly
my consumption of alcoholic beverages would be greatly reduced.

This does not, I believe, make me out to be different than most.
It surely doesn't make me out to be an alcoholic. Nor a freak.
Nor a psychological misfit. It makes me out to be a human being.

In my ken of things, being "happy" (however you interpret that)
is a rather rare human condition. If it isn't that way with you,
I can only envy you and wish I knew your secret. With most of us,
drinking only when we are "happy" would not lead to temperance,
as the above-mentioned writer indicates in his title, but rather
to abstinence or so near abstinence that you could just about
be entitled to join the Women's Christian Temperance Union.
Have you ever seen a happy WCTU member?

For a more logical pattern of imbibing, I offer my own formula,
worded to fit today's theme. It involves two simple rules:
Rule 1: Drink only when happy, unhappy, or in that in-between limbo
in which most of us find ourselves most of the time.
Rule 2: Drink moderately.

Who needs more advice?

JANUARY, 1971

CUTTINGS

It's been rumored that some California North Coast wineries
have been making perhaps as much profit the past couple of years
from the sale of vineyard cuttings as from the sale of wine.

This may or may not be true. But one North Coast producer
told me that, while his wine sales were going very well indeed,
his returns from the sale of cuttings were "fantastic."
You can interpret that quote any way you want.

You know as well as I do that demand for varietal-named wines
has for several years been growing at a considerably faster pace
than has the supply of grapes that give them their names.
This being so, the stepped-up activity in planting new acres
to grapes that will eventually be transformed into the wanted wines
is very sound business and easily understandable.

It is particularly understandable in view of the 1970 situation,
when frost decimated the crop, forcing grape-short vintners
(and that meant practically every one of the premium wine makers)
to pay up to $525 a ton for such as Chardonnay and Cabernet.
Even the year before, when the crop was rated as sizeable,
payments for some varietal grapes hit the $500 a ton mark.

They tell me—and I believe them—that you can grow a ton
of even the sparsest bearers for considerably less than that sum.
For someone in search of an honest dollar or multiples of the same,
this is quite a lodestone and it just about guarantees that demand
for cuttings of quality vines will grow with each passing year.
So will the California acreage planted to such vines.

This is looked upon as a worrisome prospect by some.
Vineyardists who have long been providing the desired varieties
are bothered by the concept, fantastic as it currently seems,
of there being a surplus of these now much-sought-after grapes,
with a consequent drop in per ton prices.

One reason for their worry: U.C. viticulturists have come up
with a program whereby a single laboratory-nurtured grapevine
will be producing cuttings by the *million*—their word, not mine—
within a couple of years. This would make the setting out
of hundreds or even thousands of acres of Chardonnay, for example,
a simple year-after-year matter. If the land can be found.

This scares some growers. But not, I would guess, the vintners.
The prospect of being faced with adequate supplies of top grapes
is hardly to be rated a bugaboo by those whose economic future
is tied to that of premium table wine. Quite the contrary.

Who needs to sell cuttings for a living?

FEBRUARY, 1971

LOGIC

I believe in logic. Major premise, minor premise, conclusion. Recently, I used logic in a little spiel on wine when I was asked why table wines differed so in taste. My answer focused on basics. Major premise: Many grape varieties are used. Minor premise: Each variety contributes its individuality to the taste of the wine. Conclusion: Therefore each type tastes differently. Logical, no?

Trouble was, I'd misunderstood the question, which was this: "Why do wines made from the *same* grape differ in taste?

I almost answered "Nonsense" before I realized it wasn't nonsense. Varietal wines *do* vary, even when made 100% from the same grape. So I started talking logic once again. By the time I had finished, I'd about convinced my audience (and me) it was almost impossible for one bottle of a varietal wine to match its name-sake. Witness:

Item 1: A varietal grape picks up characteristics from the soil. Soils vary in composition. Therefore both grape and wine vary.

Item 2: A grape reflects climatic conditions during the season. Copy-cat climates are rare. Therefore grape A and its wine, growing here, differ from grape A and *its* wine, growing there.

Item 3: Grower practices vary. This brings major-to-minor changes to like varietal grapes. Therefore to the wines made from them.

Item 4: While vintners use their own grapes, they also buy grapes. But not always from the same growers. Therefore there are varying qualities, year by year, in a vintner's grape mix and his wine.

Items 5-6-7-etc.: Grape differences are magnified by differences in winery operations. Vinification methods, storage practices, blending concepts, filling procedures, etc., vary winery to winery. Therefore some taste differences are inevitable when comparing different brands of the same 100% varietal wine.

Items *ad infinitum*: When a wine leaves the cellar, it goes through many hands: railroader, trucker, distributor, retailer, buyer. Potential variations in the care given a wine here are infinite. Therefore—as an inevitable conclusion—some taste differences are almost certain to be found in the same wine, bottle to bottle.

When the full impact of this conclusion hit me, it disturbed me. But no longer. Once again, logic has come to my rescue. Witness: Major premise: Wines, even wines carrying the same varietal name, same year, same brand, can differ. Minor premise: such differences are responsible for much of the lore and lure of winemanship. Conclusion: Therefore thank Heaven for these differences.

That is why I believe in logic. It's so flexible.

MARCH, 1971

CRIME

I really don't feel like an incipient criminal.
Yet there are people in this country who seem determined
to persuade the nation that I'm more likely than not to commit
a lawless act some day—and probably already have done so.

The reason for their suspicions—I imbibe.

I'm not being paranoid. I know that's how they feel about me.
Don't I periodically see their reports that alcohol is "involved"
in X percent—60 percent is the popular figure—of all crime?
And aren't these reports tantamount to warning you and the world
that, since I drink, there's a very good statistical chance
I may forge your signature or steal that 1940 bottle from you?
If *you* drink, aren't they warning me and the nation about you?

The fact you and I belong to the 80 percent of American adults
who reportedly imbibe alcoholic beverages of one kind or another
(not counting Geritol and other alcohol-based tonics) satisfies me
I'm by no means a member of a minority because of my drinking.
But it doesn't end my suspicions that, simply because I imbibe,
some people are trying to down me. With statistics, no less.

Well, as one who has, in his day, juggled all kinds of statistics
with one brain tied behind him, I'm not going to stand for this.
I am going to give them back their own.

What I'm going to do is to apply, to the very facts they present,
a statistical invention of mine—mathematical translation.
Come see how it works.

Let me first take up their report that alcohol is involved
in 60 percent of U.S. crimes. I'm not going to argue against it;
I'm simply going to translate it. And here is what I get—
Alcohol is *not* involved in 40 percent of the nation's crimes.
A simple, straightforward interpretation of an oft-made statement.
Not even a WCTU member could argue with it. Right?

Now for step two, which is to apply this same straightforward
interpretation to the accepted statistic that 80 percent of all
American adults are imbibers. Here again, I have no arguments.
I merely translate. Like so: Twenty percent of American adults
are *non*-imbibers of alcohol. Who can deny the clarity of this?

Now comes the third, the final and the destructive step—
making the logical connection between these two arrived-at facts:
The non-drinking 20 percent commit 40 percent of the crimes.

This now-proved kinship between non-drinkers and criminal acts
cries out for investigation. I suggest by Congress, most of whose
members are imbibers—and therefore statistically against crime.

APRIL, 1971

209

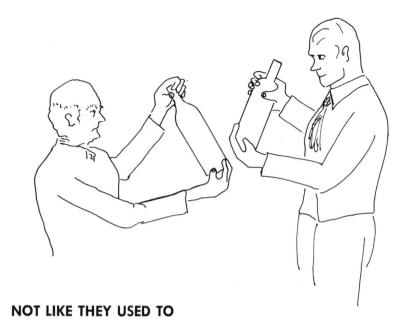

NOT LIKE THEY USED TO

"They don't make them like they used to."
This is a familiar complaint, said by many, about many things.
I've never heard it said about wine.

The reason I haven't is clear. At least to me.
The wines being made around the world today are, as a whole, better
than those made at any previous stage in the centuries-long
history of this vinous beverage.

I don't say this to belittle the winemakers of the many yesterdays
through which the industry has lived. Nor do I say it in order
to place today's winemakers on a pedestal above their predecessors.
I firmly believe the cellarmen of yore could have done everything
their counterparts of today are doing *if they had the same tools.*

By tools, I don't mean just the many mechanical and electronic
devices currently to be found in wineries around the globe,
even though I recognize the advantages these bring the winemaker.
Rather, I mean the ever-increasing body of vinicultural *knowledge*
today's winemakers have in their heads or at their finger tips.

This comes from thousands of investigations, past and present, undertaken by researchers in almost every wine producing nation, with results made available to all through technical journals. Today, winemakers not only know more about the *how* of making wine, they know more about the *why* of doing what they are doing.

This does not mean they scorn what could be called the oldest tools of winemaking — the eyes for measuring color, the nose for judging aroma and bouquet, the tongue for evaluating flavor, and particularly the memory for providing a base for judgment. These, though, are tools that man, clever as he may be, has not been able to improve, so today's winemaker has no advantage here over those who preceded him. His big plus lies in being able to bring greater sensory pleasure through a better understanding of what fermentation is and what goes on during the aging process.

That this better understanding exists, it would be silly to deny. It would be equally silly to deny its impact on cellar practices and on the resulting wines. So it is not at all surprising that a winemaker of today, dedicated to the ideal of transforming his still-to-be-harvested 1971 grapes into the best possible wine, has a much better chance of achieving this laudable goal than had his counterpart of — say — 1893 or 1937, even though the latter was equally conscientious in his winemaking efforts.

So they really *don't* make them like they used to.
The wine drinking world should be glad.

MAY, 1971

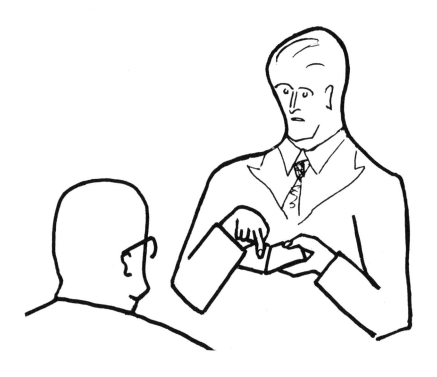

HE SAID. I SAID.

He was a tall young man with an intense look. He came up to me
at a big Champagne tasting and said, pointing, "One of the men
at that table said you might be willing to answer a beginner's
questions about Champagne." I said, "I'll try."

Referring to notes on his tasting card, he said, "Just what is
bulk process Champagne? I'm not sure I know what it means."
I said, "Well, it's a method in which the secondary fermentation
—that's the fermentation that puts the bubbles in the wine—
is carried on in a large pressure tank instead of in a bottle.
Later, the wine is filtered and bottled under pressure."

He said, "Does Champagne made this way taste different? From the kind made in the bottle, I mean." I said, "Most Champagnes differ slightly from one another, regardless of how they're made. Some people, especially those who know a lot about wine, feel certain they can tell if a Champagne is bulk or bottle fermented."

He said, "About bottle fermented Champagne." He checked his notes. "Some Champagnes have labels saying 'Fermented in the bottle' and others say 'Fermented in *this* bottle.' There's a difference?" I said, "To this extent. Where it says *this*, the Champagne was actually made in the same bottle from which it's being poured. Where it says *the*, the Champagne was simply made in *a* bottle."

He said, "That's the only difference?" I said, "No," and explained about disgorging and the bottle transfer method. He said, "Is one way better than the other?" I said, "You can get opinions on both sides." He said, "That's not very definitive." I said nothing.

He looked at his notes again. He said, "What does sparkling wine mean? Isn't Champagne a sparkling wine?" I said, "Of course." He said, "Then isn't a Sparkling Wine a Champagne?" I said, "Not necessarily," and explained the regulatory difference.

He said, "Why are some of the red wines called Sparkling Burgundy and others Champagne Rouge?" I said, "Fielder's choice." He said, "Hunh?" I said, "Two names for the same thing." He said, "Oh."

He said, "What about Cold Duck? Is that a Champagne Rouge?" I said, "No. It's different." He said, "But it's red, too." I said, "It's half Champagne, half Sparkling Burgundy." A pause.

He said, "*Brut* means dry?" I said, "Right." He said, "As dry as Extra Dry?" I said, "Drier." He said, "*Sec* means dry?" I said, "Yes." He said, "Drier than . . .?" I said, "Less dry than either."

A long pause this time. He scanned his tasting card. He said, "Which of the Champagnes that are here do you consider the best?" I said, "Excuse me. I have an appointment."

JUNE, 1971

A LAST WORD

DURING my writing career, which reaches from the composition class in my high school junior year more than four decades ago, to the day on which I am typing this out on an old Underwood (the electric typewriter is too much for me), I've always been conscious of the fact that the measure of good writing is that of getting a thought, an impression, an *idea* across to the reader.

Whether I have succeeded or failed with you in the ideas presented on the preceding pages is something I'll never know.

Maybe it's just as well.

Recently, I came across what must have been my first bit of writing about wine—a quatrain which, as I recall, I contrived for some English class at the University of California. This was back in the days when life at Berkeley was simpler (and so, apparently, were the students, if these four lines are any measure). At any rate, since this volume represents selected writings of mine about wine, I don't see any particular harm in including my first piece on the subject. Here it is.

> They say that wine and laughing ladies
> Will make me end up deep in Hades.
> But if the wine and girls are there,
> I can't see why they think I'd care.

There is no indication on the paper I found as to what mark I got on this bit of verse. I'm probably better off not knowing. But no matter what the prof thought of it, I'm sure that at the time I wrote it I liked it.

I still do.

Irving H. Marcus

WINE PUBLICATIONS

96 Parnassus Road
Berkeley, California 94708